The Gift of Unconditional Love

Fulfilling The Spiritual Dimension Of Life

Kelley

Peace & Blessing

Ed

Ed Rubenstein, Ph.D.

Published by LotusHeart Publishing
255 Sages Way, Marshall, NC 28753-5711
Copyright 2018 by Ed Rubenstein, Ph.D.

Cover and Text design by: Sandi Tomlin-Sutker

ISBN: 978-0-9668700-5-3
Library Congress Control Number: 2017919343

Website: heartbased.org
Email Address: ed@heartbased.org

This email can be used for contacting the author, exploring research possibilities, or training opportunities. This
email can also be used for information regarding large
book orders.

Printed on Demand by
Lightning Source, an INGRAM Content Group Company

Acknowledgments

I would like to thank everyone who has participated in any of the trainings offered by the Heart Based Institute. Of great and continued inspiration to me is your presence and willingness to realize how relying on the True Source of Unconditional Love brings great joy, opens our hearts, and heals our deepest wounds. Thanks to Sam Sutker, Kath Durand, Sexton, Kathy Cronin Grant, Stephanie Bloom, Jim Van Huysse, John Faherty, Christina Dupuch, Kurt Valle, Diana Stone, Sally Mydlowec, Deborah Lafon, Al Rubenstein, Carol Lokitz, Millie Levin, and Martha Atkinson for their support and suggestions. Also thanks to Sandi Tomlin-Sutker for designing and formatting. My deep thanks to Irmansyah Effendi for helping me realize that our heart's connection to the True Source of Unconditional Love can give us the best of the best. I am grateful for my wife Paramjit and two sons Arun and Sage for sharing their beautiful hearts in so many ways.

Dedicated to Heart Based Institute, a 501(c)(3) nonprofit organization, committed to educate people that our hearts are the doorway to our deepest healing, and the key to our deepest peace, calm, joy and gratitude. See page 155 to learn more.

Table of Contents

Introduction

The Gift of Unconditional Love is a self-help book in story form that teaches usable lessons based on enjoying the great gift we have been given, our hearts. Our heart is special because it is the center of peace, love, joy and happiness. It is the key to mental, emotional and spiritual growth. It is through the doorway of our heart that we can access our innate wisdom, an inner knowing we can rely on for clarity, guidance and insight.

Most of us already know the importance of our heart, because we grew up hearing, "follow your heart" and "listen to your heart." We may have also heard about the importance of, "knowing something from the depth or core of our heart". When a person does something "whole heartedly" or "puts his whole heart into it", we trust that they have given their best intentions. When we talk about meaningful communication, we know it is about having a "heart to heart" with someone. We wouldn't say I am going to have a "head to head". We often describe admirable people as having a "huge heart" or a "heart of gold". When we refer to gratitude, it is always "heartfelt gratitude". Head- or brain- felt gratitude just doesn't feel right.

Take a moment to reflect back on the most special times in your life, a time in which you felt deeply touched, especially grateful or connected to life – perhaps the birth of a child, a tranquil moment in nature, a peak experience or a time of spiritual communion. When you reflect back on those precious moments, how does it feel if you point to your head and say, "I was so touched"? Even your head knows this does not compute. However, it is natural to put your hand on your chest, and feel how you were deeply touched by that special moment. What is it that made that moment so special above the rest? It wasn't just the external circumstance. In that moment, the special and precious feeling was your direct connection with your heart. How is it that two people can experience the exact same circumstances without experiencing the same special feeling? The difference…one person experiences it from their head rather than their heart.

Over the entire span of our life, when all is said and done, it is these heartfelt experiences that provide the greatest sense of satisfaction, and joy.

We are meant to live a heart-centered life, so that we live life to the fullest with abundant love and joy. This can only happen when our heart and mind are in proper alignment and working together as a team for our highest good.. To live life with a dominant mind is to live a limited life. Our heart is the key for making each moment the most special and precious gift it can be.

Thinking or believing we are in our hearts is very different than the direct experience of being connected to our hearts. Furthermore, we cannot "follow our heart" from our brain and we cannot use our head to get into our heart. Most people have never received proper guidance or education on how to enjoy all the benefits that our heart offers. Many people often think they are already deeply connected to their heart. In reality they are only experiencing a minute fraction of what is available. It's like looking at the tip of an iceberg and not realizing that the tip is a very small part of the iceberg itself.

Our heart is the doorway to embrace the spiritual dimension of life because the core of our heart is connected to the True Source of Unconditional Love. This terminology is used as a "Universal" reference because our hearts connection to Unconditional Love exists for every person, regardless of culture, belief or religious preference. Since the Source of Unconditional Love is unlimited, and without any discrimination or conditions (or else it would not be Unconditional), it is referred to as the True Source of Unconditional Love.

Experiencing the peace, joy, love and gratitude of our hearts is actually a simple process. Unfortunately, due to our conditioning, many people believe living with a dominant mind is normal, since it is all they have ever known. When the mind is dominant, we tend to judge people or categorize them such as 'good enough' or 'not good enough', 'like' or 'dislike', 'approve' or 'disapprove' or find them 'worthy' or 'unworthy'. We can also become overcritical of others and ourselves. When our heart and mind are properly aligned and our hearts open, we become less emotionally reactive, more accepting of our own shortcomings, as well as those of others. We easily forgive and experience more gratitude, contentment and true joy in our life.

Even people with a history of traumatic life challenges can learn to easily enjoy their heart's connection with the True Source of Unconditional Love. And this connection can be utilized to dissolve, and heal long standing trauma and unresolved issues.

Truly living a heart-centered life has a profound healing effect on all levels of our being. No matter what anyone's past may be, this is something reachable and achievable for all of us. As you learn in this story, it is indeed our birthright to experience the Gift of Love... and you will also come to understand why the title of this book is The Gift of Unconditional Love. This book was written as a tool for understanding that an open heart is the safest place to be, and the key to our happiness and fulfillment. Deep in our hearts, we all know it's time to let Love give us the best of the best so that we can awaken to be who we truly are. This is meant to be a natural process so that we can fulfill the spiritual dimension of life and live how we are designed to be.

In order to integrate important key life lessons explored in the book, fifty self-reflection questions are included and can be enjoyed individually, in book clubs, or as part of a group designed to enhance well-being and spiritual fulfillment.

Chapter One
WHY, WHY, WHY?

"Oh, my God, he's dead!" I wasn't sure whether I wanted to cry, or if I felt re- lieved. I had to go into the house to tell my mother, "Dad's dead."

My name is Adam and this is the story of how I awoke from the dream of the world – a trance that controlled my thinking, my behavior, my relationships, and my future – a trance that influenced every aspect of my life, and a trance of which I was completely unaware. Believing my feelings and thoughts were normal, I was really out of touch with the depth of my pain and the agony of my separation. Thinking that getting my buttons pushed, viewing people as below or above me, and living with so many judgments about myself and others, was the way I experienced life.

A shocking sequence of events took place in my life when I was about to turn twenty-one. One day, during an argument with my father, I lost my cool and shouted at him, "Why don't you just drop dead!" I turned and walked away while he was still yelling at me. Dad always seemed angry and somehow disap- pointed with me. He put me down constantly and never had anything encour- aging to say.

Two days later dad had a heart attack in our driveway. I ran over to him, began CPR and felt him take his last breath. His body went limp as I was kneeling there holding his lifeless shoulders. His face was gray. His eyes were staring at me blankly. He was gone.

A short time after, I began having the same dream over and over again. It seemed so real. In the dream, I was standing at the entrance to our living room and my dad was sitting on the couch. He was dead but he didn't even know it and no one would tell him. It was my responsibility but I was so scared that every time I was about to tell him, I woke up in a cold sweat.

My father was still alive inside of me, it seemed. I could hear his voice in my head telling me that I was not good enough. Believing this, it felt as if his voice had become part of my voice. I was extremely confused. One part of me wished that he had never died. Another part of me felt relieved that this man who put me down so frequently, would never be able to do that again. Oh, I felt terribly guilty and ashamed for having a part of me that was glad he was dead.

I was trying not to think about my father's death, so I spent my time hanging out with friends. We were caught up in our own world of partying. I was so

1

confused but I dared not tell anyone what I was going through. I never talked about the dreams or my feelings - my sadness that he was dead, my relief and even happiness that this man I had so greatly feared was out of my life forever. The few tears I shed were tears of confusion. The whole awful scene and my role in the drama, left me in an internal state of shock.

I was constantly worrying about what others thought of me, but I didn't like my-self, my feelings, or what I saw when looking in the mirror. No one was aware of it because I played a great game and knew how to act cool. Hurting and confused on the inside, not knowing who I really was, or what life was about, I just wanted to be liked.

One night when I was out with some friends, we were drinking liquor that Fred had taken from his father's liquor cabinet. His father who was always drunk, never figured out that his son was stealing his booze. We went out for a ride in Fred's Volkswagen Bug. He was so wasted, he couldn't have walked a straight line, let alone drive a car.

Usually I would sit up front with Fred, and another friend, Bill, would take the back seat. But this time I decided to be a nice guy and give up my front seat to Bill.

We came to an intersection that had a green light, but no green arrow. Fred was so drunk he couldn't tell the difference. He made a left turn across the highway without yielding to oncoming traffic. Looking over my right shoulder I saw headlights in my face. The impact of the collision completely crushed the passenger-side door. Time came to a standstill. In an instant I saw everything that had ever happened in my life flash before my eyes. My injuries put me in the hospital for ten days. Bill didn't make it.

By this time, my mother and I were not getting along very well at all. College was out for the summer and she did not approve of the crazy guys I was hang-ing around with. I knew she was in pain over the death of my father, and was struggling to work a full-time job to make ends meet. Still, I argued with her over even the smallest of things.

Late one night it hit me all at once. It was my fault Bill was dead. I had given him my seat. My heart felt tormented by the thought that somehow I was respon-sible for both Bill and my dad's death. The pain was unbearable. Completely in despair, from deep down in my heart, I called out and begged for help. Crying, "God – who, what and wherever you are, please help me! Help me to make sense of all this pain I'm feeling. I feel so lost and alone. God, please help me to find my way Home!"

Everything suddenly became very still. It reminded me of the quiet on a snowy day when everything is covered in white. A wave of peace I never felt before came over me. A face came into my mind, as crisp and clear as any image could be. It was the face of a white-haired, bearded old man. There were dark streaks in his hair and beard. His eyes were clear and glimmering. His presence was comforting. He smiled and said, "I am Grandfather."

I wanted to think this was some kind of sign that maybe something good was going to happen, but I was afraid my imagination was playing games. As the days passed, I doubted it more and more. Life went on as usual, and I was more confused than ever. Why, why, why?

Chapter Two
A WAY OUT

My mother's growing concern finally prompted her to confide in her friend, Gabriella, an old woman she'd met at the grocery store. She told Gabriella about the friction between us, and about my refusal to see a counselor. Mom explained her fears about the dead-end track I was on, and of the hurt and anger I was trying to hide. The constant worry and physical stress brought about by our arguments was keeping Mom up at nights.

Gabriella suggested that maybe what I really needed was an opportunity to get away from the city for awhile, and that perhaps spending some time with nature would allow me to get to know myself in a deeper way. She told my mother about a remote cabin in the mountains that she and her husband, Sage, had built for themselves for that very reason.

"Sage is getting old", Gabriella said, and had been looking for someone to help out with repairs on the cabin. He had postponed his plans to put in some new fences and build a shed because he had not been able to find anyone who was available to work. Gabriella suggested to my mother the possibility of my spending the rest of the summer with Sage at the cabin. It would cost me nothing to stay there and I could even make a little money. My mother told her I would never agree to such a plan, and that prying me away from my friends would be impossible.

This was on a Friday evening and I was downtown with a group of guys hanging out across from an all-girls' private school. I didn't realize that one of the crazy guys in the group was picking a lock and trying to break into a store. An alarm tripped and everybody ran except stupid me. Hearing the alarm, I walked over to see what it was.

At that moment, a police car pulled up and a police officer looked me straight in the eye. Knowing they would think it was me that broke into the store, I ran. Fortunately I could run really fast when I was scared. With every step my stomach cramped with a sickening feeling. One of my biggest fears was getting busted for something I hadn't done.

Making it all the way home did not get rid of the fear. The police were patrolling the neighborhood and I knew they were looking for me. Mom was surprised to see me home so early and wanted to know what was up. I couldn't bring myself to tell her what had happened and tried desperately to change the subject. I mumbled something about getting out of town for awhile. "What a stupid thing to say!" I thought. It was impossible. We couldn't afford any trips, and besides, where else was there to go?

I looked up and saw that my mom had a big smile on her face. It was the first time she had smiled in months. Then she told me about Gabriella and their conversation earlier that evening. It sounded like a crazy idea – hanging out with some old geezer out in the middle of nowhere but I had no choice, so I agreed to give it a try. Little did I know where this adventure would bring me.

Chapter Three
GETTING THERE

The next morning Gabriella stopped by with a map and directions explaining how to find the cabin, which they had named the LotusHeart Cabin. What a relief to leave town after a restless night filled with dreams about cops chasing me.

I threw some clothes in a backpack and slipped into my mother's car with a hat pulled down to my eyes. When at last we passed through the city limits, a tremendous weight lifted from my shoulders. I breathed a huge sigh of relief.

After a few hours of driving, my mother dropped me off at the end of a dirt road surrounded by trees. There wasn't a house, or even another person, anywhere in sight. I had to walk up a winding trail to get to Sage's cabin. It was a great feeling walking through the forest. Alone, and free, no cops would ever find me out here.

By the time I approached the cabin it was late afternoon. I saw an old man on the front porch sitting in a rocking chair. As our eyes met, I stopped, dead in my tracks and shook my head in disbelief. There was no denying that Sage was the white-haired old man whose face I had seen when crying out to God for help. He even had the black streaks in his gray hair and beard. Shaking in my shoes, thinking "this can't be," I wondered if my mind was playing tricks on me again.

"Welcome, Adam," he said. "Grandmother Gabriella told me you might be coming."

"You're Grandfather Sage," I said.

"Yes, Adam. Some people call me 'Grandfather.' But I have been known by other names. "

I was stunned and told him, "I had a dream and saw a face that looked just like you and heard the words, 'I am Grandfather'."

"Well, isn't that a coincidence," he said. "I saw you in a dream, and now here you are, right before my eyes."

"Who is this old man? Is he making fun of me?," I wondered.

"So what should I call you?" I asked, trying to be cool about this weird 'coincidence'.

"You can call me whatever you like."

"How 'bout if I just call you 'Gramps?' "

"That will be fine, Adam. If I am your grandfather, then that would make you my grandson. But actually you are my brother." He walked over and put his hand on my shoulder. "You know, Adam," he said, "You are a student just like me. We are siblings and pilgrims passing through life. Welcome to the LotusHeart schoolhouse. Welcome to the classroom of life."

Chapter Four
EARTH SCHOOL

After a good night's sleep I was awakened by the old man singing a song about letting your heart shine and letting the love flow. It felt natural to hear him sing even though it seemed like a scene out of some kind of fairy tale.

The cabin was quite primitive. I had been told that Gabriella and Sage had built it with logs from trees on the land. I glanced around, but couldn't find a clock. Nor could I find Grandfather Sage. He had disappeared.

I went outside to look around. There was a large herb and vegetable garden on the south side of the cabin, and beyond that a small orchard. A beautiful river and waterfall flowed nearby.

I'd been used to sleeping in late at home, and realized this would not be part of my routine here with ol' Gramps. He got up with the sun. Sitting down on the front porch steps, I wondered if coming here had been a mistake. There wasn't really much to do. Then Grandfather came walking up the hill from the river.

"Ready for breakfast, Adam?"

Gramps sat in silence for a few minutes before he started eating. I asked him what he was doing and he replied that he was feeling heartfelt gratitude to the Creator for providing such blessings in the form of the food we were about to eat. I noticed he did not like to talk while eating. He chewed each bite slowly and embraced each mouthful as if he had never tasted food before.

My habit was to gulp my food down as quickly as possible. I was getting impatient just watching him. He must have known what I was thinking because he smiled and said, "You will get over it and one day you may even enjoy eating with gratitude."

Grabbing a bunch of grapes to pop in my mouth, Gramps stopped me. He suggested I slow down, relax, smile, and let my heart give thanks to the True Source of Unconditional Love for the grapes and all the wonderful things in my life. However, at that time I couldn't think of much to be grateful for besides the grapes. I did think things were starting to get a little weird, but I decided to do my best to have an open mind, be honest and not play games with the old man.

"So, Gramps," I asked, when we had finished eating, "what exactly did you mean last night when you said I'm a 'student?' I'm out of college for the summer and I don't intend to do any studying."

"What if I told you we are always in school, wherever we are, and whatever we are doing?" he asked.

"Hey, man, what are you trying to tell me? The whole world is a classroom, or what?" I asked, laughing.

"Exactly, Adam! Life becomes much more interesting and exciting when you understand that your life itself is your great teacher and your classroom. What if I told you that you are on earth to learn to become who you really are, not to remain who you think or believe you are or what other people have told you about yourself or want you to be. Unless you learn to live a heart-centered life, with your heart and mind in alignment, you will never be able to find the real you."

Wow! What he said touched something deep inside of me and I felt a wonderful sense of relief. Another part of me felt scared and very cautious. What if this guy is crazy and tries to convince me of his weird ways?

Chapter Five
FALLING IN HOLES

I found out that I was dead wrong about there not being much to do. It was time to go to work. Grandfather wanted to replace some old fence posts so we dug out the old posts and replaced them with new ones. When we finished the job a few hours later, he asked me, "Adam, how would you like me to show you the biography of many people's lives?"

"I'm not sure what you mean," I replied.

He asked me to grab a shovel and I followed him down a path about a hundred yards from the cabin. He instructed me to dig a hole about two feet wide and one foot deep. I started digging, wondering what he was up to. Gramps leaned against a tree and closed his eyes while he waited, looking as peaceful as a baby in the arms of its mother. He seemed to be from another planet.

After I finished digging the hole, Gramps asked me to have a seat where he had been standing. " This is an old story that I'm going to act out for you. You are the audience and you are going to see the role that many people play in the theater of life. Adam are you ready for the first scene?"

"Go for it, Gramps."

Walking down the path Gramps stepped into the hole.

"How did that hole get there?" he asked.

Stepping out of the hole Gramps walked back to the beginning of the path.

"Now, Adam. Let me show you the next scene." The old man walked down the path and stepped into the hole again.

Asking irritably Gramps exclaimed, "Why doesn't someone fix that hole?"

In the next scene he walked down the path and fell in the hole again. "That stupid hole!" he exclaimed loudly. "It should not be there. Who is responsible for this hole in the path?"

Gramps walked over to me then, and said, "This is the condition of many people's lives. They repeat mistakes over and over again. They find fault with others or blame someone else so they do not have to take personal responsibility for their mistakes. They keep falling in the same old hole."

"We all have lessons to learn Adam, and we continue to fall into the same holes until we learn the lessons. When we come to realize that falling in these holes is creating pain and misery in our lives, we learn to change."

"I know what you mean, but that doesn't apply to me," I said.

"Let me show you the next scene," he said, walking back to the beginning of the path. This time, Gramps looked at the hole, but still fell in.

"It is not always easy to avoid the hole, even when we know it is there. The next scene goes like this." He walked down the path, looked the hole and almost fell in, but then stepped to the side and missed it.

To demonstrate the next scene, Gramps walked down the path and saw the hole way in advance, walked around it and didn't even come close to falling in.

"Adam, what do you think the last scene is?"

I didn't know.

He turned around and took off on a different path. I grabbed the shovel and ran to catch up with him.

"Go back and fill up the hole so we don't fall in again." He placed a hand on my shoulder and stared into my eyes. "With lots of paths, and so many holes, it is important to be able to see where you are walking. Adam, you are going to learn how to be on your path while experiencing the awakening of the real you. This will happen by allowing the gentleness of Love to open your heart."

"Why do you have to be different than everyone else?" I blurted out. "I am not even sure there is a God, and what is this nonsense about love. Letting your guard down will burn you. I have been there, and you can't tell me different."

"Adam, I can understand how you feel, because I had similar thoughts when I was a young man and got rejected by the girl I thought I was going to marry. But the True Source of Love will never hurt you and is always present to give us the best of the best. We do not live in separation from one another. The core of our heart is connected to a field of Love beyond us. That is why humanity is our family and you are my brother."

"Gramps, you are spooking me out. Don't put any pressure on me. What is this nonsense about the source of love? I only believe something if I see it, and all I see around me is a world that looks like it is going to hell. I sure do not see the love you are talking about."

"How about you will believe it when you feel it and know it in your heart?" Gramps remarked.

"Gotta think about that one Gramps." Wow, this guy was hard to figure out. He sure seemed weird.

Chapter Six
CLOSER THAN WE THINK

Later that day we hiked up a nearby mountain to reach a feeding station Grandfather maintained for the deer in the area.

"Now, Adam," he said, as we walked, "I would like to share with you a little of my own story. We have more in common than you think."

I couldn't imagine having anything in common with this old man. After all, he was over seventy years old.

"Adam, when I was seventeen I was very confused. My father was not a good teacher or role model because he was unsure of the purpose of his own life. Daddy did not know how to give me guidance about how to live a peaceful, balanced life. Like you, I grew up living with fear and intimidation rather than love and support."

"And, like you, I was affected by peer pressure. Compromising my own values got me into trouble. I was told repeatedly that I would never amount to anything and over time began to believe it. As a result, I got into even more trouble."

"Many of my friends ended up in jail. They, too, felt that they were not worthy of good things and happiness. They had come to believe the negative messages they were given about themselves. Words like 'you are not good enough' eventually turn into 'I am not good enough.'" He paused, and his normally sparkling eyes became dark and sad. I felt kind of sorry for him.

"I hear you, Gramps. Those kinds of messages can be like a tape playing over and over in your head."

"I was fortunate," he continued, "because someone came along who helped me to see those past negative experiences as a gift – a gift that has allowed me to learn, grow and teach others. It was my own pain that helped me to understand the pain that squelches the hearts of so many people. The pain in peoples' lives is a result of living a mind dominant life and believing their 'head' is supposed to guide their life. When the brain is the boss, the heart is closed. I am so grateful to realize that I can only know my true self in the core of my heart. Adam, if you do not allow your heart to open, you will never have lasting happiness."

"What do you mean Gramps? Are you telling me what I see, hear, smell, touch and think is not real? Sounds like you are living in a make believe fairy land with all this heart stuff. I've been happy lots of times."

"I'm glad to hear that Adam. Have you given any thought to the destiny of your brain?"

"The destiny of my brain is _____" I drew a blank.

Gramps smiled and with a happy laugh replied, "The destiny of your brain is the graveyard. All brains go to the graveyard. No one gets to skip this," he chuckled. "Adam, are you ready to open your heart? The real you is deep within your heart and the quality of your heart will determine the quality of your life and your relationships. This is central to a calm, joyful, loving and happy life. The connection between your heart and the True Source of Unconditional Love is the key."

Not knowing what to say and feeling a bit in shock, I could not get the image about my brain crumbling to dust in a graveyard out of my mind. Suddenly I heard myself thinking, "There is no way I am going to open my heart. The last time my heart opened for this girl, I got hurt, chewed up and spit out."

Chapter Seven
THE FOUNDATION IS BUILT

I was very curious about all the handmade crafts in the cabin and wondered what was in the antique cabinet next to the woodstove. I opened the cabinet door a couple of inches to peek inside, and Grandfather walked in.

"Snooping around, eh? Anything I can help you with?"

"Well, I was... I mean, I was..."

"Cat got your tongue, Adam? I have a sense you were feeling sneaky and you got caught. Boy, I used to hate that when it happened to me."

Embarrassed, I was at a loss for words.

"I... I'm so sorry... "

"Adam, I have nothing to hide. You are welcome to look around all you like. It feels kind of fun, though, to think you are getting away with something you're not supposed to do, doesn't it? I know what that sneaky feeling feels like and how it plays with your head."

That evening we built a campfire and sat, staring into the flames for what seemed to be hours. The silence was beginning to get to me, and finally I asked Grandfather if he would tell me more about the classroom of life.

"Let's begin with you," he said. "Be willing to look at yourself honestly. Realize your emotional patterns and how you react to the environment. How do you deal with things when they do not go the way you want? How do you judge others and yourself? What excuses do you come up with to justify your right to become angry, upset or disgruntled? You will learn that what you see and how you react to the world outside of you is a mirror of your inner world

"Hey, wait a minute Gramps. Are you telling me I am crazy? What I see is what I see, and what I know is what I know."

"Adam, I understand your position. Feels like I hit a nerve inside of you, so let's just let things chill a bit. I trust that what I shared will make more sense to you as we get to know each other. Life has many lessons for us to learn."

I was glad that he was not trying to push me because I did not like getting pushed. "So Gramps, how do you go about learning these lessons you're talking about?"

"Fortunately, life sees to it that we get to work out all our lessons," he chuckled, and got up to put more wood on the fire.

I asked Grandfather why it is so difficult for people to change, even though they think the change might be good for them. He asked me what I thought.

"Well, I guess they are afraid of change," I said.

"Yes, fear is part of it. People oftentimes feel safe and familiar with their old ways, even though those old ways create mental discomfort or emotional pain. We may have a fear of letting go because we don't know what will happen when we do. Does a tree fear letting go of its leaves when winter comes? Then, Adam, why do we fear letting go of old patterns that we have outgrown? Why would you want to resist removing a painful thorn that is under your skin?"

That's heavy, I thought. It sounded weird, but I think I knew what he meant because something deep inside me said, "Wow!"

With a piercing gaze he stared into my eyes and said, "Adam, there is an innate longing in the core of every being to feel profoundly safe and unconditionally loved. People often end up on dangerous dead end roads because of misdirected attempts to fulfill that innate longing that is within us. Searching for happiness and love in the wrong places can lead to addiction, or thinking that money, sex, name, fame, power or material possessions can bring spiritual contentment. Our heart is the doorway to the fulfillment of our innate longing because the core of our heart is connected to the True Source of Unconditional Love."

Something in what he said made sense to me. I could see the dangerous dead end street that led to several friends of mine overdosing and dying from pain pills. I told Grandfather about that and he said, "Many people are self-medicating with alcohol or drugs because they are in a lot of emotional pain. They do not know how to get relief in any other way. Unfortunately, they do not realize yet that our heart is the doorway to fulfilling our innate longing and the key to dissolving deep unresolved guilt, shame, unworthiness and even the parts of us that feel unlovable.

Gramps stared into the fire for several minutes before he spoke again. "I will share with you, Adam, five principles which I would like you to consider as the foundation of learning in the classroom of life. Please just listen and do not talk until I am done telling you what they are."

Number One:

"The True Source of Unconditional Love is the Source of our true heart feelings.

Adam, peace, joy, love, gratitude, gentleness, warmth and expansiveness are our true heart feelings and these are the natural expressions of our heart. We are not the originator of these feelings. True heart feelings exist because we are connected to something that is beyond ourselves. As our hearts open more and more, we realize that our heart is connected to the True Source of Love.

Number Two:

"The True Source of Unconditional Love is the Source of our life

Life is not just about us. We are part of a unity. Adam, the more that we are able to rely on the connection between our heart and the Source of Unconditional Love, we realize that this connection to the core or our heart is the Source of our life. This is an intimate relationship that embraces the core of our being, and is more than what our mind alone could possibly experience.

Number Three:

"The True Source of Unconditional Love is always present to give us the best

Feeling the true heart feelings and enjoying heart-felt gratitude allows our connection to the Source of Love to grow. Adam, this allows our heart to open even more and we receive so many benefits in all aspects of our life. The ease of feeling and enjoying this most beautiful heart connection is our birthright, no matter what we have ever done, or whatever our circumstances may be. The Gift of Unconditional Love is not something received by proving our worthiness or earning it from our actions. It is freely given, always present and available to all... and that is why it is a Gift beyond all gifts.

Number Four:

"Our deepest purpose on earth is to be an instrument through our connection with the True Source of Unconditional Love

"Adam, as we let our hearts open by feeling the true heart feelings, our old baggage starts to melt away. Complaints, grudges, resentments and issues are dissolved by the Unconditional Love from the Source of Love and this sets our heart free. We become more grateful and happy to effortlessly be an instrument so that the gentleness of Love freely radiates without us having to do anything to let that happen naturally.

Number Five:

"Living a heart-centered life and relying on the True Source of Unconditional Love, will bring us Home to who we really are.

"We are meant to fulfill the spiritual dimension of life through the doorway of our heart. Adam, only by living a heart-centered life can we truly wake up. "

"Gramps, are you telling me I am sleeping? And why are you so caught up on this gift of love stuff. I learned in school that everything is energy, so why don't you just call it all energy? Your talking weird, flakey and mushy crap and that's not how we talk in my neighborhood."

"I hear you Adam. It is a stretch to grasp, and I can understand how it can push your buttons."

Grandfather went on to explain that a part of us may still want to think that our connection to that beyond our separateness is an energetic connection, or a symbiotic relationship with nature. However, our heart can directly realize that the connection that links us beyond our self-created world is much more than an energetic connection. Just as our heart is touched when we see a mother breast feeding her child, we instinctively know that this is a bond of love, not energy. And that which bonds us to the Source of life, is the Gift of Unconditional Love. He went on to explain that when one truly opens their heart, they realize that their connection to life is not about energy, it is about profound Unconditional Love, beyond what the mind could possibly grasp. I was shocked that tears welled up in my eyes when he told me that we can learn to live a heart-centered life with the security, comfort and safety that a baby feels being hugged in the arms of its mom. I quickly shut the tears down, but was surprised because I hardly even shed a tear when my father died.

"Adam, as you learn to feel true heart feelings and rely on the True Source of Unconditional Love, your heart will open in all directions. The peace, gratitude and joy in your life will be experienced beyond your wildest dreams. Even if the world around you becomes chaotic, you can remain calm and centered in your heart. You will not be shaken by life's troubles."

"Grandfather, would you write down the five principles for me in the journal you gave me?"

When we returned to the cabin that night, I read them again and again and thought about them. One part of me thought that "The Five Principles" were a joke and I could not see how these principles would actually work in my world where I would have to focus and work hard to get what I wanted out of life. Another part said, "Wow, wouldn't this be awesome if these principles were real and Gramps is not a nut?"

Chapter Eight
OUR HEART SPEAKS

After breakfast the next morning we went down to the river with wheelbarrows to collect some stones for landscaping around the cabin. After filling our wheelbarrows, Grandfather sat down and said, "Let's take a break."

"Adam, I want you to try something. Close your eyes and tell me what you hear?" Over the low roar of the rushing river, I became aware of the more subtle sounds of trickling and bubbling as the water passed between the rocks, which I hadn't heard before. We sat quietly just listening for several minutes.

Then Grandfather spoke. "Our heart has a voice, Adam, and it is always speaking to us. When we do not know how to listen, we can not follow our heart."

"Really, what does this voice of our heart sound like? Does it sound like Moses or my mother lecturing me?" I asked jokingly.

"Well Adam, I can promise you that if it sounds like either of them, it is not your heart speaking." He laughed and then became quiet and firm in his communication. "First you must be open and willing to feel your heart. If your head tells you that this is all silly, then you have already closed yourself off to the key to life and the key to happiness."

"Speaking of keys, Gramps, if I had a key to a new car, and a key to a nice place to live, along with a really pretty girlfriend, I would have it made."

"I can understand that," said Grandfather lightly "and I used to have my own version of what I thought would make me happy. I am grateful to realize now that the keys I thought would lead to happiness actually got me locked in a dark closet. Adam, your heart can learn many things through circumstances, experiences, and all of your relationships."

"Do you mean like I can learn something from you, Gramps?"

"Adam, I'm not so sure you are even taking my words seriously and hear sarcasm in your tone, but I will continue anyway. Many times in my life, circumstances have found me. In other words, I was not consciously looking to meet a certain person, but they showed up at the right time, for an important reason. Each time, my heart learned something beneficial from them, or an answer to a question or problem was revealed."

"My brother, life speaks to us through other people's pain. We can learn what not to do by observing the painful lessons of others. We can also learn from the imperfections that others may display. Strange but true, there is even more to learn from our emotional reactions to their imperfections." Gramps thought that one was really funny. "If we do not learn from others imperfections, Adam, then it may also become our ignorance. When we do not learn our lessons, we end up suffering as well. We are capable of falling into the same hole that they did."

"Yah, I can see that. I have fallen into the same kind of holes as my friends."

"The voice of life that often becomes our greatest teacher is our own pain, Adam. I am talking about mental and emotional pain. Your pain acts as a signal to inform you that you are not in harmony, and you are certainly not in your heart. It tells you that you are stuck in your head. When you learn to live from your heart it will save you enormous grief and problems."

"I don't think I have what it takes to live from my heart," I said. "By the way, I don't personally think that is a safe way to live your life. I mean, I'm not even sure it is a good idea."

"Adam! Wake up! You are in an old hole!," Grandfather exclaimed. He got my attention and snapped me out of my daze. "What is life telling you now, Adam?"

"I can't hear anything, Gramps."

"Do you realize you are so stuck living in your head that this is creating all of the discomfort in your life?" he asked. "Are you aware that you are living in your own self-created soap opera and have come to believe it as real? That is just a story you created in the world of your mind."

I didn't know what to say but felt that what he said rang true.

"What's so fascinating to me, Adam, is that life has a way of arranging things so that lessons keep reappearing in different forms. We cannot get away from them. Wherever we go, life will be there waiting for us with similar problems and the same lessons until we have learned them. Developing insight and realizations from your heart will help you recognize the gifts from the lessons life is offering you."

Feeling less skeptical, I asked, "How do you do that Grandfather? Will you show me?"

"Alright Adam, now we can get somewhere! My heart can now feel your sincerity and openness to learn."

"I can't promise you I will buy everything you say about the heart, but let's give it a try," I replied.

"First you have to learn how to feel, enjoy and allow your heart to open. The heart we are talking about is not your physical heart. This is your non-physical heart and it is located at the center of your chest."

"How do you know it is real if it is non-physical," I asked.

"Well, the mind cannot be found under an x-ray or MRI machine, but you know you have one."

"I'm glad its a non-physical heart," I said "cause I am not in the mood for opening up my physical heart. That would be painful!" I chuckled.

"Don't worry about it being painful because when you open your heart it will feel very nice. It will be better than chocolate, ice cream, mangoes and pizza."

"Yeah right, I will believe that when I feel it or taste it. Can we start now?"

"OK...Touch your heart in the center of your chest with a couple of fingers. This will improve the attention to your heart. Now close your eyes to reduce the domination of your brain. Relax ... and smile. Now smile to your heart without thinking about where or how so your heart and feeling grow stronger. Now Adam, feel the calm, peaceful feeling in your heart. Follow that nice feeling."

"This is ridiculous," I blurted out as I opened my eyes with a groan. "Next thing you are going to want me to do is dance in a dress and put on ballet shoes. Are you training me to be a sissy? Why are you so obsessed with this heart stuff? Give me a break Gramps."

"Sounds like I pushed your buttons Adam. That doesn't surprise me. I bet you learned in the school yard to fight or get angry but you were never taught how to feel."

"Only sissy's feel. They get emotional and they get picked on and beat up all the time. That's not me! I don't have to take crap from anybody."

"Well Adam, sounds like it's time to eat some watermelon. There is a cold one waiting for us in the cabin."

Chapter Nine
TRUE HEART FEELINGS ARE NOT EMOTIONS

I decided not to play games with Gramps, and was going to tell him exactly what I thought even if he did not want to hear it. What did I get myself into? Would it be better if I just ran off to have some fun with my friends? Gramps seemed to know something was cooking with me.

"Well Adam, wasn't that a tasty sweet watermelon?"

"Look Gramps, enough of this heart stuff. It doesn't work for me. You have no idea about my world. I don't want to get emotional and am not interested in opening my heart. I opened my heart to this girl I loved, it hurt so bad when she left me, and I swore I'd never open my heart again. You just live in some fantasy world out here in the woods."

"Adam, I believe you have never really opened your heart."

"Don't tell me what I have done. I loved Janet so much, she meant the world to me, and I would have done anything for her."

"Actually, that's not opening your heart. That is opening your emotions to another person. Your attachment and possessiveness of her is what created all of your hurt and anger. When you truly open your heart, you do not get hurt like you previously did because the connection between your heart and the True Source of Love is established."

"Why should I want to feel, if feeling is painful?" I asked.

"Adam, emotions and feelings are not the same. Whether you want to accept it or not, on a daily basis we create many emotions such as disappointments, frustrations, worry, anxiety, as well as resentments. Do you know why?"

"No, but I expect you are going to tell me it's because I live in my head."

"Yes, painful emotions and judgments are created and contaminate the field of your heart when your mind is dominant. When you are centered in your heart, you do not create emotional reactivity to situations. You remain calm even in the storms of life. Your buttons don't get pushed the way they do when you are mind dominant."

"So what's this big difference you talk about between emotions and feelings? It all seems the same to me."

"As I said, emotions are created when you are head centered. Your head goes into reaction because of thoughts and unresolved memories which activate emotions. Unlike emotions, true heart feelings are the natural byproduct of your heart. These feelings of lightness, expansion, calmness, peacefulness, joy, gratitude and love radiate when you feel them, because our heart is connected to the Source of Love, the Source of our life. The main reason that you do not feel the wonderful feelings is because you are stuck in your head. I am not interested in you getting emotional Adam. I am only interested in you waking up and learning enjoy all of the benefits your heart's connection offers."

Grandfather paused and then asked, "Is it possible to be happy and ungrateful at the same time?"

"I have to think about that one Gramps."

"Come on now young man, that's a no brainer".

"Well I guess in order to be happy you have to be grateful."

"Yes Adam, and it is heart felt gratitude, not mind or brain gratitude. True happiness is from the heart and nowhere else. Don't be fooled to think otherwise."

A part of me understood what he said. There was a definite peace, calm and happiness that radiated from Grandfather, and I wondered if it was possible for me to ever feel that.

Grandfather continued quietly, "A little while ago, you told me you didn't believe in this heart stuff and that I lived in a fantasy land. Do I have permission to tell you what I think?"

"Gramps, I think you are setting me up. But go ahead anyway."

"I think the reason that you are resisting this 'heart stuff' is because a part of you is scared."

"What do you mean scared? This is nothing compared to when I was jumped by three guys."

"Adam, it's about the fear of the unknown and your fear of loosing control. It is also about not trusting what might happen if you allow your heart to open. Are you ready to begin facing your fear or would you rather hide and make believe your fear does not exist?"

At first I got angry. "I knew you were setting me up!" I shouted, but couldn't help laughing when I saw the smirk on Gramp's face.

"Okay Adam, round two. Touch your heart, close your eyes, relax, and smile."

Grandfather guided me to let go of the muscle tension and guarding I was holding in my body. The layers of tension dissolved, and he then had me smile to my heart without thinking where or how. When he asked me to feel, I began to sense a feeling of lightness, peace and calm. He instructed me to follow the feeling by enjoying the feeling. The more I felt the feeling, the more the expansive, calm, and peaceful feeling grew. I opened my eyes and felt quite surprised thinking, "maybe there really is something to this 'heart stuff'. "

Chapter Ten
SUNSHINE NOT FELT

We were relaxing in the cabin later that day when Grandfather asked me to step outside in order to give him a weather report.

"Adam, can you tell me if the sun is out?"

"It's cloudy. The sun's not out."

He raised his voice and exclaimed, "Look outside again and tell me if the sun is out!"

I went back outside but nothing had changed. What's he getting at now? Can't he see the sun isn't out? "Hey, Gramps, I'm sorry to disappoint you, but not only are there white clouds, there are also dark gray clouds. You can look up at the sky all you want, but you won't get any sun on your face."

Grandfather smiled with a childish grin.

I know that smile, I mumbled to myself. He's up to something. What is it and what is the message here?

"Lots of clouds, sunshine not felt," he said.

"That's what I said, Gramps."

"No, it's not Adam."

"Yes, it is."

"No, it's not," he repeated quietly.

I started getting angry.

"No, it's not," Grandfather said again, laughing.

"Yes, it is!" I insisted.

"Go outside, Adam, and look again."

I walked out and came back in. "Okay, you win, lots of clouds, sunshine not felt."

He jumped up and shouted, "You got it, my brother!"

"C'mon, Gramps," I said, still frustrated. "What's going on here?"

"What is the difference between your first report and what you said just now?" he asked. "Let's go outside, Adam, and sit quietly. Reflect over what happened and you will realize one of the most important lessons life is offering us."

We sat on the ground and leaned against a tree. I didn't get it. He closed his eyes. I could see a shining radiance in his face. "Wow, there's a lot of sunshine in him," I thought. Then it dawned on me. The reason he appeared to be so full of light is because he didn't have clouds blocking his sun, and his heart was radiating from his connection to the Source of Love. I remembered my first comment – "the sun's not out."

"Wait a minute Gramps. The sun's always out, or we'd be in a lot of trouble on this planet. The sun's always shining, but we don't feel the sunshine when it's blocked by clouds. With light clouds we feel some warmth, but with heavy, dark clouds we feel no sunshine at all even though the sun is still there."

"You've got it partly," he said, "but not fully. The clouds in your mind did not just blow in from the north or south like the clouds in the sky. If they did, we would all be at the mercy of the wind. This means we would be helpless victims without the power to choose and create. We create the clouds when we live in our heads and our mind is dominant. They are not created when we are within our hearts. Adam, there are some stubborn storm clouds hanging around your heart that keep you from feeling the depth of profound joy and love. You created those clouds when your head was dominant. Don't worry, we will return to visit those darker clouds another time."

"I'm not sure I want to."

"No problem Adam. Everything will unfold in its due time"

"And do not forget that you create your own weather. The biggest trap is thinking the clouds just roll in without your permission. You always have a choice to be in your heart instead of your head.

"Adam, do you understand how these messages from nature apply to our lives?"

"Well, I think so. The sun represents the core of my heart, where I'm connected to the True Source of Love. The clouds are like the holes I keep falling into, and the negative thoughts and emotions my mind creates. These clouds don't just blow in. The clouds are the patterns of emotional and mental discomfort that I create. Is that right, Gramps?"

Saying with surprise, "You mean you have actually been listening with an open heart, Adam?"

"I hear it and understand it. It's a great way to live out here in the woods, but I'm not so sure it would work in my world."

Chapter Eleven
WEEDING

The next morning we spent a few hours working in the vegetable garden, which supplied us with much of our food.

"Adam, as we stand in this garden now, the voice of life is speaking to you," said Grandfather.

My first thought was that the spinach and lettuce didn't have much for brains. Grandfather winked at me. He knew just how to read me.

"To be honest, I'm not sure what the connection is between me and your garden except that it gives us food to eat," I said.

"Adam, if we look, feel and listen, we can grasp a deeper metaphor of what the garden represents in our lives."

He asked me to sit with him in the center of the garden, to be silent and experience what was going on there.

"What do you observe Adam?"

"I see cucumbers, tomatoes, broccoli, squash, lettuce, and watermelon. I also see a bunch of weeds starting to grow Gramps. Looks like you have gotten behind in your weeding."

"Well young man, these weeds growing are for you and you will get to eat them later in your salad."

"What are you talking about; we don't eat weeds where I come from. The weed over there has prickles and thorns and that would tear up our mouths. I tell you what Gramps, why don't you eat the weeds and I'll eat the lettuce and the cucumbers. You can have my portion of weeds in your salad."

Grandfather was acting pretty serious, and I would not put anything past him. I thought, "Maybe this guy really likes eating thorny weeds."

"What Adam, you don't want to eat the weeds? Come on now, I thought that was your favorite food."

"Huh," I exclaimed?

"You eat weeds throughout the day and relish them like desert."

"What are you talking about Gramps?"

"The weeds of your mind, Adam. You feast on them and you don't even know it. When you live with a dominant mind, weeds grow and you eat them through-out the day. Not only that, you become just like the weeds and at times even grow thorns."

He caught me by surprise. I tried to speak but began to stutter.

Grandfather continued," Our mind creates a variety of weeds along with rea-sons and excuses about why we have a right to be angry, upset, judgmental, burdened or disturbed. Then we act justified as if it is okay to keep having these negativities toward ourselves or other people. We may also blame circumstanc-es for why we don't feel good."

Grandfather laughed as he explained, "People can even think they are bene-fiting from their excuses because now they have a reason to think and believe they are justified to be mad, upset, or burdened. The mind can actually keep convincing them to stay identified with those negative emotions for years to come."

"Look Gramps, there is this older guy in my neighborhood who has treated me like crap since I was a kid. I have a right to be angry at him, and I am not going to let it go because he deserves it."

"So Adam, who is the one who suffers from all of your resentments?"

"I don't care if I have resentments toward him because he deserves the worst of the worst. You don't understand how he has treated me all these years."

"Adam, we will deal with your resentments another time. Sounds like this weed developed a deep root system," Grandfather chuckled. "For now let's get back to the vegetables and watermelon. Your heart is not capable of growing weeds. The food that nourishes your being and supports you to be happy and truly successful is grown in the garden of your heart."

"I don't understand or buy what you are saying, Gramps. You are trying to tell me that my mind is bad and if my mind was such a terrible thing, why was I born with a brain?"

"Adam, I happen to like my brain, and would not be able to be here talking to you if I did not have one. Actually, the problem is not the brain. The problem occurs when we let the dominant mind be the director. When the brain and mind are overly dominant, the heart remains closed. Then we are disconnected from our greatest gift and treasure, our hearts. When we allow ourselves to be heart-centered, the brain becomes a friend in helping us carry out the orders of our heart. We make positive choices and feel good at the same time. Then, even though you are using your brain, you don't create weeds because your heart is dominant. You can never dirty your heart when you are in your heart. You only contaminate your heart when you are in your head creating excuses for your right to get emotionally reactive."

"By making your heart contaminated, do you mean the storm clouds that block the radiance of the sun shining through?" I asked.

Grandfather smiled and nodded because he realized that I understood. He went on to explain that I had layers of old storm clouds blocking the inner most radiance of my heart. Until these blockages were dissolved I would not be able to experience the sublime gentleness and intimate joyful connection between my heart and the Source of Love.

"So, Adam, what is the best way to tend to the garden of your heart?"

"When I learn to live a heart-centered life, I won't create any new weeds and then only have to pull out the ones created by living in my head, right?"

"Yes Adam, but one more important thing. You don't want to pull the weeds. There is a better way."

"So who will pull the weeds if I don't?"

Grandfather seemed to find my confusion humorous. He remarked, "Lets save that for another time. When the time is right, I will show you the best and easiest way to get rid of your weeds and storm clouds."

Feeling a knot in the pit of my gut, I was both scared and relieved at the same time.

Chapter Twelve
RELAX, SMILE AND ENJOY

After lunch we walked a short distance through the woods to a beautiful, still pond situated near an open meadow. Grandfather told me the surrounding area was a bird sanctuary. He shook one of the trees and a number of birds began flying overhead.

"What is the voice of life communicating to us now, Adam?"

I didn't have the foggiest idea. "Birds fly, and I can't."

Gramps laughed. "What are the birds showing you?" he asked.

"They are showing me they can fly," I replied.

"Yes, my brother, they can fly. And where are they flying?"

"The birds are flying over our heads."

"That is correct, and what conclusion can you come to from this observation?"

"I'm stuck on this one, Gramps."

Getting a very serious expression on his face while looking straight into my eyes, he said, "You may not be able to keep a bird from flying over your head, but you can sure prevent it from building a nest in your hair."

We both burst out in laughter.

"How did you expect me to figure that one out?"

"I didn't, Adam. But maybe we can translate this experience into a useful insight."

My mind began to race looking for an answer.

"You will not get the answer from your intellect. Let's sit in silence until you get it. Allow your heart to tell you."

We sat down and after a while I began to worry because nothing was coming to me. I knew he would be willing to sit there until midnight, if necessary. Grandfather loved his silence. I became increasingly impatient.

"I don't think you are going to get it by sitting there squirming," said Grandfather. "How about you relax, smile, and enjoy the nice feelings from your heart and the insight will be revealed to you."

Thoughts of different sorts poured into my mind. I let them go and continued to sit quietly. Then some memories about the guy who had wrecked my motor bike and never even apologized came to my mind. I felt anger brewing inside of me and became aware of the negative emotions still being stored, even though this happened several years ago. Letting go of all muscle tensions and smiling to my heart, I began to enjoy the calm, peaceful feeling that began to expand in my chest.

"Got it! When living in my head, the bird can build a nest in my hair. Then she starts laying eggs and before long I have a whole family up there. Getting stuck in my head won't happen if I also learn how to be in my heart. Negative thoughts and emotions will come and go, but they won't nestle or make my head their home. I allowed this guy who wrecked my motor bike to build a nest in my head, and the anger from that is still there even though it happened years ago."

"Yes!" Grandfather said with a radiant smile. "Look, everything we have been talking about over the last few days is a process. You and I are still in process. You are not going to get it all at once, though it is important to have proper understanding. Then you can begin to build a solid foundation. As you get to experience being in your heart more and more, the less you'll be stuck in your head. You will experience deeper joy in each moment and there will be less and less drama created from living in your head. The more you are in your heart, the less you will experience anger, disappointment, worry, frustration, and burdens. The question is whether or not you invite those thoughts and emotions to be permanent guests, give them a bed to sleep in and food to eat."

"I guess we don't want them to get so comfortable they don't want to leave or think that my head is their home."

"Exactly Adam."

We laughed again.

Chapter Thirteen
BRAINWASHED BY SOCIETY

It rained that night and most of the next day. Grandfather kept busy in the cabin – first, chopping vegetables to make a pot of soup, then wiping down all the shelves in the kitchen, then repairing the handle on an old garden rake.

He brought out a collection of arrowheads he had found in the area to let me look at them. One arrowhead in particular caught my eye. Thinking I could make a necklace out of it when I got back home, I slipped it into my pocket. I thought he would never miss it considering how many he had. Wow, I really made up a good excuse to justify my actions.

Grandfather finally settled into his rocking chair in front of the woodstove. As he closed his eyes and began to smile his face became radiant and I could tell he was really enjoying himself. After putting the arrowhead collection away and looking through all the magazines in the cabin, I sat staring out the window.

The forest looked beautiful, with a foggy mist moving gracefully through the treetops. Still, I couldn't help wondering when the rain might stop. Grandfather opened his eyes and looked up at me.

"You know, Adam, life will never be perfect if you judge it in terms of how things are looking on the outside. Contentment is a state of being that only your heart can truly know."

"The world, in many ways, is a mess because when people live in their head, they get self-centered and self-righteous. They create divisions. As a result people hurt one another, damage the environment, and find all kinds of ways to justify their behavior. They search for happiness in the wrong places. In many ways, that's what so many different types of addiction are about. Different addictions, whether it be alcohol, drugs, gambling, promiscuity, or greed are a misdirected attempt to find happiness outside of themselves. All along, what they are really looking for is closer than close."

"Their heart," I exclaimed.

"Adam, even in nature things are not perfect. Too much sun, you burn. Bee stings hurt, thorns prick. The world cannot give you contentment. If you do not find the sweetness of contentment in your heart, then the outside world will always seem like there are problems. But when you learn to experience contentment within, you can enjoy the world because you do not expect your happiness to come from the world. The connection of your heart to the True Source of Love will bring the deepest level of happiness."

"Adam, do you realize you have been brainwashed by society?"

"What do mean by brainwashed?" I asked.

"You can think of it as a conditioning process. And some of this conditioning has been good. That means it supports and nourishes the development of the positive you."

"I know what you're getting at now, Gramps. You're saying I've also been negatively conditioned, and it's interfering with my ability to be, as you say, 'content within'."

"That's right, Adam. It is often convenient to blame someone or something else in our lives for not being happy or content. These excuses are a cop-out. When we use excuses, Adam, we are forgetting that we, ourselves, are responsible for being content."

"Yah Gramps, I get it. It's like when I used to blame my father for just about everything. After he died I started blaming my mother, or the school, if things didn't turn out right."

"The mistake we often make," said Grandfather, "is we look to achieve happiness from external things, experiences, or other people. That's a trap."

I looked out the window again and thought about the values of my peer group. I asked myself, "Where do my friends think happiness comes from?" It was very clear that sex and money are the things they think they need to have in order to be happy. I explained this to Grandfather.

"Do you believe that, Adam?" he asked.

"Well, yes, I guess I've thought the same thing, but now it does sound kind of funny."

"Yes, Adam. Sex and money are the cosmic joke. Depending on them for contentment will send you on a wild goose chase. There is no saying where that ride could lead you, but one thing is sure – it is a dead end road. People have been falling in that hole and getting themselves in trouble throughout the history of humankind."

Grandfather continued, "Do not buy into the negative conditioning that tries to tell you success is what you have or possess. True success is based upon a deep connection between your heart and the Gift of Unconditional Love, the Source of your life. Your quality of life depends upon the quality of your heart connection. When you feel the true heart feelings more and more, your connection to the Source of Love will open your heart bigger and bigger. This will set you free as you learn to live a heart-centered life. "

He closed his eyes again with that radiant smile and I could tell he was bathing in a joy and contentment. I continued to sit quietly, watching the trees through the window and felt guilty as I fingered the arrowhead in my pocket.

Chapter Fourteen
OBSTACLES ARE OPPORTUNITIES

The rain stopped late in the afternoon. We went for a hike and decided to rest in an area that had been hit quite hard by a storm the previous winter. Grandfather asked me to look around and tell him what I saw. It was easy to see that many trees were lying uprooted on the ground.

"There is an important lesson here to learn," Grandfather said, and asked me if I could discover the insight. "Your hint, Adam, is to closely study the fallen trees, and then study the trees still standing. Why is it that certain trees survived the storm while others did not? Is that just a coincidence?"

I wandered through the forest comparing the trees. I noticed the trees that had toppled over had shallow root systems. Those trees that were rigid, and not able to bend and flow with the storm, were snapped in half. The trees which were well-rooted and flexible were able to bend and adjust to the weather conditions.

"Guess we're supposed to live our lives like the trees that are still standing – being strong, flexible and well-rooted," I said.

"This is true, Adam, and it is good to be rooted as long as you are rooted in your heart and not your head. Be committed to your foundation. Don't be persuaded by some of the nonsense that your head will tell you because that will lead you away from your heart. Also be flexible like the oak tree to bend in the storms of life. We are in process of spiritual enfoldment and change may call us to new and deeper realizations. If we are rigid, we get stuck and miss out. When we are flexible, we bounce back when the storms of life hit us. If you are rigid, you break easily under pressure."

Thinking about what Grandfather said regarding the importance of being well-rooted, I remembered how frequently my behaviors mimicked my friends. Casually going along with whatever my friends wanted to do, I didn't develop my own root system. I realized that without learning this lesson, I could be influenced again and again, and the storms of life would blow me over. My face must have shown my lack of confidence to change.

"Lighten up, Adam, and enjoy the ride. Storms will come and go. It is an inevitable part of the nature of life. People will disappoint you at times. You will see the acts of other people's ignorance, and their ignorance may affect you or your loved ones. Not only that, your imperfections may affect others at times. Give the world permission to be imperfect," he continued. "Guess what, Adam? There will be times when you get knocked down, or thrown from the horse, so to speak."

"What do you do then?" I asked.

"Do you want to lose your horse, Adam?"

"No."

"Then what might you choose to do?"

"I better brush myself off and get back on the horse," I replied.

"Exactly, and that is just what you do in life. You get out of your head, and back into your heart. When you choose to feel the true heart feelings and return to your heart, it means you got back on your horse. Adam, I have another secret for you. When you fall off the horse, or you get knocked down, there is always a gift waiting for you. You are given the opportunity to enjoy and value your heart. Then you learn to trust the innate wisdom of your heart. This will help you learn many realizations about life and the bigger purpose of why we exist. Now that is a great gift. Could it be that you allowed yourself to be thrown from the horse? It is also important to integrate the new realizations you have received, and learn from it, so it does not happen again."

"Are you saying, Gramps, that obstacles can be our friends? I have a problem with that. I see them as a pain in the ass."

"If we treat obstacles as our enemies, life will be an uphill battle. If you greet obstacles as opportunities for your heart to learn, you can have fun even when the going gets rough."

"That's easier said than done, Gramps."

"Adam, you are absolutely correct. I choose to keep reminding myself, though, that obstacles are my opportunities. I have a tendency to sometimes forget this, especially when I am in the middle of them," he said, laughing at himself. "I make it sound easy, perhaps, but believe me, Adam, my life has been quite a ride with lots of challenges along the way. I am so grateful that I now realize the True Source of Love is always giving me the best of the best, and we have been unconditionally loved in every moment of our existence. Be patient and enjoy the ride. When your heart truly realizes how you have been Loved unconditionally, you will never be the same again."

"I hear what you're saying, and it makes some sense but I still think you're out to lunch about how problems can be your opportunities. And this idea of being loved completely, I am not there."

"I hear you brother, and understand why you think that."

Chapter Fifteen
METAMORPHOSIS

On our way back to the cabin, we stopped at a raspberry patch and ate berries as we plucked them from the bushes.

"These berries are great," I said.

"I appreciate them, too, Adam. Sometimes, to get to the sweetest berry, you have to get around the thorns. Watch where you are going."

Getting his meaning I said, "Gramps, some of the thorns of life have caught me in the butt because I wasn't watching where I was going."

Grandfather pointed out a cocoon. "What would happen if you opened up that cocoon?"

"I guess we'd see a caterpillar."

"Would it serve that caterpillar if we opened up its cocoon?"

"No. It wouldn't have a chance to become a butterfly."

"That's right, Adam. Did you know if you do not let a baby fall when it is learning to walk, it does not learn to walk as well? Adam, our lives are a metamorphosis. We are all evolving from being head centered to heart centered. Then we can fly with grace. If you do not get to experience your heart, you will remain stuck in your cocoon and never get to spread your wings."

We headed back to the cabin as the sun was starting to set. On our way we passed by a muddy pond.

"Do you see that lotus in the pond?" asked Grandfather. "It's in the mud, but its blossom is well above the mud, basking in the sun. The lotus is the symbol of Love and represents that we can live in the world but not get sucked into the drama, or mud, of the world."

"I see it but sometimes getting muddy is fun, ya know."

"It's your life, Adam. You'll play it as you choose."

We walked on, but I couldn't get his last statement out of my head. I get to play life as I choose. The arrowhead in my pocket began to feel very heavy and my guilt began to feel overwhelming. Is this really the way I'd like to play this scene? My guilt feelings seemed to overpower the pleasure I'd felt in possessing the arrowhead. Realizing that I created a crazy excuse to take the arrowhead, my heart felt to return it.   From the perspective of my heart, I never would have allowed myself to take the arrowhead. Wow, the head can play tricky games and talk me into things I shouldn't be thinking or doing.

Later, back at the cabin, when Grandfather stepped outside to split some firewood, I cautiously slipped the arrowhead back in with the rest of the collection.

Chapter Sixteen
PERSPECTIVE *FROM* THE *HEART*

The next day we went down to the river to cool off after a few hours of working in the hot sun.

"Adam, is there anything you need?" Grandfather asked.

"Sure. I need a new car, a stereo system and some new sneakers, and I need..."

"OK, that's enough, Adam."

He asked me to bend down and put my head under the water. Thinking he was challenging me, I took several deep breaths to build up my lung capacity, then went under.

After about fifty seconds I was running out of air and started to raise my head to the surface. I felt a hand behind my head, holding me down. I started to freak out. "Is he trying to kill me?" I wondered. Crying out in my mind, "I need air!" He released his hand from my head. Bursting up while gasping for air, I yelled, "What are you nuts, you could have killed me!"

"Do you need air?" he asked calmly.

"What's your point Gramps?"

"You cannot live without that which you need, Adam."

"Here we go again", I thought. "What is this guy getting at now? He sure has a strange way of making a point."

"So we agree that you need air," he continued. "Do you need a new car? And sneakers?"

"Well, not exactly, I guess."

"If you do not need them, then what is your relationship to that car?"

"I'd like to have a new car," I said.

"Exactly! Do not confuse needs with luxuries. A new car, a stereo system and sneakers are luxuries, not needs. What you would like and what you need are very different. You need air, water, food, and shelter, or you cannot survive.

When you do not have your needs met, you feel threatened, just like you did when you ran out of air under the water."

We climbed up the bank from the river and headed back to the cabin for lunch.

As we walked Gramps asked, "Adam, how would a meal taste if we used weeds instead of fresh garden vegetables?"

"I know where you're going with this question, Gramps," I replied. "You're saying when I think I really need something it is like a weed in my mind."

"Adam, you're no fun," he laughed. "I thought I was going to get to play a while longer, but you cut straight to the point. Yes, you are correct. When you think you need something, you create a feeling that something is wrong if you do not have it. Have you ever experienced that?"

"Well, it reminds me of when I was going out with Janet. I felt like I really needed her to keep going out with me. When she said she didn't want to go out with me anymore, it felt like I would die. It felt devastating, like my world had fallen apart. Even when thinking about her now, I feel pissed off at what she did to me."

"But Adam, your world did fall apart. You created a drama that said, 'I need her to keep liking me.' Your 'need' created a sense of disaster when it did not happen. Your world also started falling apart when your head was under the water, didn't it?" he asked.

"Yes, it did. Real quick!"

"The difference is you really did need air, and in a few more seconds, if you did not get any, we would have had a serious crisis on our hands," he laughed.

"Gramps, it wasn't very funny at the time."

"Your need for air was real. Your need for Janet was your self-created illusion. You really never needed her. When your head was dominant, the need was created. You believed what you created, and all this time you allowed that belief to affect you."

"I can see that," I said.

"Let's ask your heart. Touch your heart Adam, relax, smile and feel what I am asking you. How does your heart feel about needing Janet?"

"Well, my heart feels like I don't need her. It would have been nice to continue going out with her, but I guess it was not in the plans"

"Great Adam. You are beginning to realize how when faced with the same situation, you perceive things one way with your head and a different way with your heart. That answer was from your innate heart wisdom. Which one do you like better, the perception from your head of needing her or the perspective of your heart wisdom accepting that the relationship did not work out?"

"It really does feel so different from my heart, and I'm much more at ease."

"Exactly my friend. And when you learn to live a heart-centered life and perceive reality from the perspective of the innate wisdom of your heart, you will live in a much different world than you do now. You will feel you're looking at life through a different set of eyes and ears."

"You mean I won't look at things or hear things the same way as I do now?"

"That's right, and you will feel different as well. There will be so much more calm, peace, light, joy, and feelings of expansion. Most of all, there will be a feeling of being loved completely, and that is beyond your mind's capacity to comprehend."

Chapter Seventeen
TAKE THE COMPASS

Feeling restless after an early supper that evening, I decided to hike out into the woods to do a little exploring. Grandfather warned me that if I ventured into the forest beyond the feeding station there would not be any more trails. He suggested I take his compass if wandering deep into the woods, or else finding my way back could be difficult. I laughed.

Who does he think he is, to insinuate that I don't have enough common sense to find my way back? When I reached the end of the trail, I thought hiking for just a few more minutes couldn't make it hard to find my way back.

It was incredibly refreshing to be out on my own for a change. I walked into a grove of ancient-looking trees and sat down to rest. My mind wandered back to the city, and my friends. While I was wondering what they'd say if they could see me now, hearing rolling thunder in the distance brought me back to the present. I decided to head back.

I stood up and saw dark clouds moving in, heard thunder again, and saw a flash of lightning. It started to rain so I started running back toward the cabin. The thunder sounded like a bowling alley and shook the ground as I ran. The rain began to pour. Running until I was out of breath, I ducked under a tree to rest for a moment. I suddenly realized that the feeding station was not in site. I had been running the wrong way!!

I started to get really scared. Lightning was flashing all around me. I curled up in a fetal position under the tree and put my arms over my head. I had never been more frightened in my life. The rain and lightning storm lasted for what must have been hours. It eventually settled down to a hard steady drizzle, but by then it was pitch black. I was cold and my t-shirt and shorts were soaking wet. Hearing coyotes howling from somewhere in the distance, I thought they were coming to get me. Thinking I would either be eaten or shiver to death from the cold, it was the longest night of my life. I was petrified with fear.

Feeling extremely relieved when the sun began to rise, I felt so grateful that I was still alive. I got up and started running. Even though I didn't know where I was going, it made me feel less lost and running through the woods helped me warm up. I came to a dirt road and followed it. My heart jumped with joy after realizing the main road that led to Grandfather's trailhead was just ahead.

When I got back I found Grandfather sitting on the porch in the morning sun, peeling an apple.

"I guess you forgot to take the compass," he said, smiling.

"Very funny, Gramps. You've got a weird sense of humor."

"I am glad you were not eaten, Adam. The bob cats and coyotes are hungry this time of year. If you had not shown up by eight this morning, I was going to have a search and rescue squad go looking for you. I'll bet you were scared up there in that lightning storm, having to spend the night in the wilderness and all."

"It wasn't too bad," I said. "I actually had a pretty good time."

"I'm glad to hear that, Adam. I was concerned you may have been frightened."

"I'm tougher than you think, Gramps."

"I guess I didn't realize how tough you are, Adam. Oh, I was just wondering, when you made the decision to not take the compass, were you in your head or heart? Just for the fun of it, close your eyes and remember how you felt when I asked you to take the compass."

I was quickly able to realize that I was in my head and in a really stubborn mood. Feeling resistant to his suggestion, I thought he was treating me like a child. Thinking, "don't tell me what to do!" got me into a lot of trouble.

"Okay Gramps, I get the point. My head was in charge."

"Adam, for a short experiment, close your eyes, relax, smile and enjoy the true heart feelings radiating from your heart. Relax more, and now just feel how your heart would have responded when I suggested that you take the compass."

I could sense a totally different response - feeling, "Maybe it would be a good idea to take the compass just in case I need it. It fits easily in my pocket. How nice of Gramps to be concerned."

"Isn't it interesting, Adam, that the head and the heart can look at the same event in such different ways? How would your life be if it was guided by the innate wisdom of your heart instead of your head?"

"Gramps are you trying to brainwash me? I am not ready to give up my head."

"Wonderful Adam, that's as it should be. I am only suggesting that your heart lead your head, instead of your head thinking it is the boss. You are free to let your head think and act as if it is the boss, though if you choose to do so, you will miss out on the greatest gift and opportunity you have. And that is an intimate joyous connection with the True Source of Unconditional Love."

At this point, it was just an idea to me because I could not feel a deep connection. I could feel some calm and peace when relaxing and smiling to my heart, though what he was talking about seemed so far away.

Chapter Eighteen
SURVIVAL MECHANISM

Later that morning Grandfather suggested we go into the woods to track some animals. "Not to hurt them, Adam, but to study them," he said. "Your task is to observe how an animal reacts when you do your very best to catch it."

Going back out into the woods was the last thing I wanted to do, and I had a hunch he was well aware of it. I didn't have the nerve to say anything though, after telling him that I had "a pretty good time", and got ready to go.

After an hour or so of hiking, we came to a small clearing. On a nearby hill we could see a couple of deer grazing. As we approached, they sensed our presence. One of the deer looked over her shoulder at us, and they both took off as if they were running for their lives.

We resumed our hike, and several minutes later Grandfather asked me, "What do you think those deer are doing now?"

"They are most likely grazing on the other side of the hill."

"Exactly, Adam."

Next we saw some wild turkeys. When we tried to go near them, they took off like they thought they were going to end up on somebody's Thanksgiving table.

"I never knew a groundhog could move so fast until trying to catch one," said Grandfather. "What is going on with these animals, Adam?"

"They feel the need to escape," I said.

"What would happen if we cornered them, and they could not get away?" Grandfather asked.

"I guess they would put up a pretty good fight, even to their death."

"Yes, they would. Do you know what this response is called, Adam?"

"I think it's the survival mechanism."

"Right. Another name for it is the fight or flight response. When animals are faced with danger, they either fight, flight or freeze up. One of two things happen: they either lose the fight and die, or they get away. If they get away, what do you think they do next?"

"Well, Gramps, I don't think they're getting an ulcer wondering if we're on their trail."

"That's right. Adam, is this survival mechanism bad or good?"

"It's good."

"Actually it can be both," he said.

"I remember my own survival mechanism kicking in one time," I said. "Last year a group of older guys gave me a hard time and embarrassed me in front of my friends. Some months later I saw them across the street. It had snowed, and I was sort of showing off for my friends. I threw a snowball across the street with all my might. Unfortunately, one of those guys got his head in the way and the snowball creamed him. He fell to his knees for a moment, and I knew his brain must have been in shock. Boy, was he pissed. He came running over with a group of five big guys, angrier than a bat out of hell. One of my friends yelled, 'Run!' I took off. They chased me, but they couldn't catch me. I ran faster than I ever have in my life. Within seconds, I climbed over a huge fence. If it wasn't for that fight/flight response, I would have been hurting pretty badly when those guys caught up with me. That's why I think the survival mechanism is good. I think it saved my life that time."

"Adam, my survival mechanism has also saved me several times in my life. It also gave me the strength to help save others when the need arose. This is the good part of the survival mechanism. It is surely there for an important reason.

"I know you told me," he went on, "that spending the night out in that lightning storm was no problem, but are you sure your fight-flight response wasn't activated even just a little bit?"

"Well, maybe a little, Gramps."

"That's funny, because when checking in with my heart last night, I could feel your mind was racing and you were really scared."

I wondered if he was playing games. Or could he really "tune in" to me?

Chapter Nineteen
FEELING TRUE HEART FEELINGS

When we returned to the cabin we saw two rabbits munching on lettuce in the garden. I started toward them to chase them away, but Grandfather stopped me.

"There is enough to feed the four of us," he chuckled. We sat down on the front porch steps to watch the rabbits while we rested from our hike.

"Adam, why do you think you, me and animals have a survival mechanism?"

"So we can survive."

"When does our survival mechanism become activated?" he asked.

"When we feel threatened."

"Exactly, Adam, but there are different degrees of activation of this mechanism."

"You mean at times we may feel only a little threatened, and other times we may feel extremely threatened?" I asked.

"That's right. Most people live with at least an ongoing low grade activation of their fight/flight mechanism. They do not ever get to the point in feeling 'I have arrived and everything is wonderful'. They are on the go to the next thing and the next thing. Often, even if everything seems okay, there is a part of them waiting for the other shoe to drop. Or they seem to always think about what comes next."

"I can really understand that because that is what my life feels like. Feels like I'm always trying to get somewhere, but I never reach my destination. It also feels like there is something missing, something I'm supposed to do or become, and that feeling never goes away."

"Adam there is something missing."

"What's that?" I asked.

"I am not going to tell you because I know that you know."

Like a flash, I understood that what was missing was the experiential connection between my heart and the True Source of Unconditional Love. A part of me realized that without having a deep connection, I would always be looking or searching for something. Grandfather could tell that I understood.

"You're not alone, Adam. This is the predicament that humans face. It's looking for fulfillment in the wrong places or in a limited way. That's why there is activation in the fight/flight mechanism even though no real threat is at hand. It is very rare that we are being harmfully threatened. But when our dominant mind is our center, we will continue to experience an incompleteness and feeling of separation. Only through the doorway of our heart can we be complete and bridge the divide of separateness that humans feel. Unless you learn to enjoy the true heart feelings of your heart, you will be running on the treadmill, uphill."

"Okay Gramps, this is the deal. When I touch my heart, relax and smile, I can feel a nice feeling of peace and calm but nothing like you are feeling. When I look at you when you're smiling to your heart, I can tell you are connected to something so big and the joy radiates through you. It's like glowing from your face. I have never seen anything like that before. How come I can't do it like that?"

"You can Adam. I have just been smiling to my heart a little longer than you have. Let's see if we can realize why you are not feeling more than you are now."

Grandfather had me close my eyes and relax deeply. He guided me to smile to my heart, and feel the beautiful true heart feelings. I could feel the calm and peaceful feeling but nothing like how he was able to feel.

"Adam, stay in the nice feeling and keep feeling the wonderful feelings. What happens when you keep relaxing and feeling the nice feelings?"

"The calm, peace, light and expansive feeling grows stronger. It feels like my heart is opening," I whispered.

"Exactly Adam, the more you feel the true heart feelings, the more your heart opens. Feeling the true heart feelings is the way we communicate with the True Source of Unconditional Love, the Source of our life. Feeling and being grateful is our way of saying yes, so the gentleness of Love can flow and open our hearts more. We can't do it by our effort. It is the gift of our connection that opens our heart."

"You mean all I have to do is keep feeling the true heart feelings, and the rest will happen for me? How can it be that simple?"

Grandfather let out a big sigh of relief and seemed so happy to hear about my realization.

"Adam, it is that simple but you are not feeling the peace, calm and joy as much as you think you are. I will show you what I mean. Keep feeling the true heart feelings, and let me know how much of you is feeling and how much of you is not."

"I can feel a part of me in the heart enjoying the nice feeling, and I can also feel a big part of me in my head, looking down at the part of me in the heart"

"Great insight Adam. Another time we can discuss your insight about how a big part of you is in your head observing your heart instead of simply enjoying your heart. But for now how about you step into the shoes of that scared young man who just realized he hit a bully in the head with a snowball?"

Within seconds, I began to feel the fear I had felt on that day. My heart started to speed up, and I got a knot in my stomach.

"What happened after the snowball hit him, Adam?"

"I ran fast."

"What was that like?"

"Like running for my life."

"Well, you were running for your life, and I know you were glad he didn't catch you," Grandfather laughed.

"I can really feel how all of me is now in my head," I responded.

"Adam, you had a good reason to have full blown fight/flight activation because you were in danger. Now you have to learn how to separate real danger from make believe danger. The main point," said Grandfather, "is that just because you feel defensive, or threatened, or unsafe, does not necessarily mean you are actually in danger. Now, those feelings may be there for a good reason. You or someone else may really be in danger. Your house could be on fire, there could have been a car wreck, a tornado could be nearby, you're being attacked or you have to run fast to help someone. These are good reasons for your survival mechanism to be activated, and that is what it is designed to do. The fight/flight response helps us to help ourselves, or others, during very difficult or threatening circumstances."

"Well, Gramps, the deer also ran for a good reason. They have probably seen many of their buddies get bumped off by hunters."

"That's right, Adam. But when the danger is eliminated, they go back to grazing."

"Seems like many humans have forgotten how to graze," I said.

"Absolutely. Peoples burdens, worrying, or feeling unsafe in relationships can keep this fight or flight response activated."

"So, if I want to graze and not be constantly on the run, I better learn to get out of my head and into my heart?"

Grandfather smiled and replied, "And it is the only way you will be happy and fulfilled in your life."

Chapter Twenty
OBSERVING AND TRYING

While we were doing the dishes that night, I said, "Grandfather, you never really answered my question. Why do you feel so much more than I do, and why my face does not radiate and glow the way yours does?"

"You answered your own question Adam. You just did not realize it. You were aware that there was one part of you in your heart, and a big part of you in your head observing the part of you in your heart. Is that so?"

"Yes, but what does that have to do with it?" I asked.

"Adam, that part of your mind that is observing the part of you that is enjoying the true heart feelings, is the part that does not yet trust your heart. So you are maintaining a separation, and it feels safer to your mind to observe from a distance. You have a fear of loosing control of who you think you are. You have failed to realize that who you think you are is a very limited story."

"But what will happen to me, if I let all of me come into my heart?" I asked.

"You will become more of whom you really are and less of who you are not. You will experience heartfulness and learn to live a heart-centered life. Adam, aren't you able to feel how wonderful it is to feel your heart's connection?"

"Yes I can, and I can feel calm, deep peace and a sort of gentle soft feeling."

Grandfather continued, "As you let more and more of you experience feeling the true heart feelings, the calm and peace will grow into profound joy, gratitude and love. Your heart will be touched like you have never been touched before. And submerging into the gentleness that you described is the key because love is always the most gentle and will never force us."

"So how do I stop observing and trust that it is safe to feel more?"

"It is a process that takes time. In addition to observing, you are not relaxed enough and you are trying. The part of you that is trying is the part of you that thinks you can do better than what your heart's connection to the True Source of Unconditional Love can do for you," Grandfather laughed. "I used to try harder and harder, because I thought my effort would improve the result. Then I realized how arrogant I had been to think I can improve what the Gift of Unconditional Love is waiting to give me, if I only get out of the way!"

"I hear you, but it will take me some time to digest that one. I always thought that in order to get somewhere in this life, you got to use more and more effort.

If I don't do it, no one will do it for me, you know?"

"I understand your logic Adam because I used to think the same thing. Time for us to settle down for sleep."

Chapter Twenty-One
WHAT'S DONE IS DONE

One morning as we were just about to begin some repair work on the roof of the cabin, Grandfather suddenly changed his plans.

"What a beautiful morning!" he exclaimed. "Life is speaking to us from every direction! I believe I hear the birds calling us down to the river. Let's go, Adam!"

We put our tools away and walked downstream until we came to a shady spot where a beautiful green moss covered the rocks like a plush carpeting. We sat on the ground where we could feel rays of sunshine through the branches of the trees, warming our skin.

Grandfather got up and walked away. He returned a few minutes later with a dead butterfly and a dead ladybug he had found.

"Open your hand, Adam. I would like you to hold these." He placed the butterfly and the ladybug in my palm.

"What would you like me to do? Bury them?"

"I would like you to bring them back to life."

"How can I do that? They're dead."

"Go ahead. Try, and see what happens," Grandfather continued.

"I can try from now until doomsday, Gramps, but this butterfly is not going to fly out of my hands."

"Why is that?" he asked.

"Because it's a done deal. They're dead."

"I agree, Adam. A done deal is a done deal. Would it make sense to argue with a done deal and expect the circumstances to change?"

"Well, you could, Gramps, but you'd be wasting your time. Why argue or try to change a done deal? Why try to bring something back to life that's already dead?"

"Exactly. I have a question for you, Adam. Have you ever said to yourself, 'That shouldn't have happened,' or 'They shouldn't have done that to me?' "

"Well, sure. I've said that a number of times when things happen I didn't like."

"Guess what you were doing, my brother."

"I'm not sure." I reflected on the time someone had put nails in my bicycle tires. I thought he shouldn't have done it. I felt angry and irritable for days. Why did I respond that way? What was I doing? Ah-ha! I was arguing with a done deal.

"Hey, Gramps," I said, "it doesn't make sense to argue with a done deal. What's done is done."

"Right, Adam!"

"What else can you do in a situation like that?" I asked.

"How about relaxing and smiling to your heart? If you are in your heart connection, there will be much less emotional reactivity and you can accept that what is, is."

"That makes sense, I guess. You'd feel less stressed," I said with a smile. "Otherwise it's like trying to swim upstream, against the natural flow of the water."

"Good analogy, Adam. This is how people tire so quickly in life. When you argue with a done deal, you are swimming against the current. You will keep hitting your head against the situation."

We sat in silence for a few moments watching the river flow by. I decided to confide in Grandfather my guilt feelings over my father's death. That was one done deal I couldn't so easily let go.

"He died in my arms, after I had told him to drop dead," I explained. "I didn't mean it. He shouldn't have done that."

"Adam, you are carrying around the painful guilt that his death was your fault. Soon I plan to share with you a way to get rid of your guilt, resentments and other unresolved emotions that have been clouding your heart. You have been carrying around a lot of baggage regarding the relationship with your father. If you do not heal this, it will affect the rest of your life."

His words were comforting to me at first. Then I got spooked.

"What do you mean??" I gasped. "Hey, Gramps! Are you saying you talk to the dead?"

"No, relax and smile Adam, some of your stuff has come up for cleansing. And there are even more layers beyond that. The Gift of Unconditional Love is going to take care of everything and give you the best. All you have to do is relax and let the gentleness of Love work."

I heard what grandfather said, but at that time, couldn't realize the profound spiritual depth of what he had just communicated with me.

Chapter Twenty-Two
CROSSING THE LINE

Grandfather sat down to rest in his rocking chair on the front porch after we had finished our repairs on the roof. I was sitting inside the cabin thinking about my father and feeling depressed again. There was no changing what had happened. I had to put it out of my mind or knew I'd go crazy.

I got up and wandered around looking at all the old pictures hanging on the walls. There were a couple of antique shotguns hanging in one corner. I took one down and examined the intricate woodworking someone had done on the stock. All of a sudden the gun blasted and flew out of my hands, knocking me backward, into the wall.

I heard Grandfather yell. The window was blown to bits and the wall around it was completely torn up. Grandfather burst through the cabin door, his eyes bulging and blood gushing from one side of his face. He left a trail of blood on the floor as he crossed the room and grabbed a towel, applying pressure with both hands to the side of his face. His shirt was already stained red. I felt a chill go up my spine and I started to shake. I could have killed him!

"You have crossed the line, Adam," he said calmly, but I could hear the anger in his voice. "It is time for you to leave."

"It was an accident! I was just looking at it!" I yelled. "You're bleeding badly! We need to get you to the hospital!"

"I'll take care of myself," Grandfather stated.

"I won't leave you like this! Let me drive you to the hospital," I pleaded.

He agreed and we left immediately. We rushed down the trail to where his truck was parked on the dirt road. Not a word was spoken during the drive. I worried he may have been weakening from the loss of blood. What if he dies, what if he dies? The words went around and around in my head.

When we arrived at the hospital the doctors took him in right away. I stayed in the emergency room waiting area and was in a daze, just sitting and staring at the wall. I couldn't believe what was happening.

An hour later a doctor came out and told me Sage was lucky he hadn't lost the vision in his right eye. They had done minor surgery to remove the shotgun pellets, and he had required numerous stitches. The doctor said Grandfather

Sage would not tell him how it had happened. I told him it was my fault, but didn't explain anything further. Grandfather did not tell him more because it would mean getting the sheriff involved.

On the way back, Grandfather said he did not think I was mature enough to handle any more of what he wanted to share with me. When we arrived back to the LotusHeart Cabin, he wished me well and said good-bye. Then he went down to the waterfall to meditate and be by himself.

I grabbed my backpack and left. I wandered into the forest on the connecting national land. After sitting down on a rotted-out log, I began to weep.

Conflicting thoughts ran through my head. "This guy had acted like he really cared, but he didn't give a crap about me. Nobody understands me or what I've been through," I thought. I felt like the biggest loser on earth – a royal jerk and screw-up. Maybe he's right. Maybe I'm not capable of learning what he's been trying to teach me.

"Is this going to be my whole life?" I cried out not caring whether I lived.

I realized I was really stuck in my head. I remembered grandfather telling me that when we are in our head, we believe our story to be real and true. I wondered how the story and all the pain I was feeling would be if I was in my heart. I called out for help. My body was still trembling inside from what happened but I began to relax more. Smiling to my heart was still difficult. I let go more, and began to feel the nice feeling of peace and calm. Following the feeling, the calm and peace grew stronger. My heart realized that these true heart feelings existed because of my heart's connection to the True Source of Love. The feelings became more gentle and beautiful. My heart felt that I had to go back and apologize to Grandfather and ask him for another chance. I knew I could learn things from this old man that I could not find anywhere else.

I made my way back to the LotusHeart Cabin. Grandfather was still at the waterfall.

"I'd like to speak to you, Grandfather. I'm so sorry for what I did. I'm asking for your forgiveness and one more chance."

Grandfather opened his eyes and said, "Look, Adam. You are a guest in my house, and it is your responsibility to honor and respect my space. You have violated my space and that is something I will not tolerate."

"I don't know why I fell into the same hole of stupidity."

"You will continue to step into that hole, Adam, unless you are able to defuse the pattern behind it."

"What pattern is that?" I asked.

"Your pattern of thinking that says you are a failure and a loser. You attract and create circumstances to support this unconscious pattern."

"Do you mean this shooting incident is a result of my feeling that I'm a screw-up?"

"Of course. You believe it without even knowing it. And you continue to seek confirmation to prove that you are a failure or a screw up. This allows you to further validate your belief that you are a failure. When you learn to be grounded in your heart and live a heart-centered life, these self-defeating patterns will be dissolved."

"What do I do now?" I asked.

"First, figure out how you are going to fix my window and the wall. We will deal with your hole in your head later," he added with a compassionate smile.

I drove into town to get a replacement window, which I paid for with my earnings. Grandfather showed me how to install it. He also taught me about gun safety. He explained that he kept the gun loaded in case of an emergency. He had recently had to kill a rabid raccoon that had come into the yard.

Chapter Twenty-Three
WE ARE ALL A FAMILY

The following morning I was still very upset about the accident with the shotgun. Grandfather sat at the kitchen table repairing the soles on his work boots, as calm as if nothing had ever happened. He sensed my shame and reassured me he would be okay. I couldn't believe he found it so easy to forgive me. In all my life I had never known anyone like him.

I was practicing feeling my heart when we heard a commotion out in the goat shed. I jumped up and ran to the door to see what was going on.

"Ah," said Grandfather, without even looking up, "it sounds like they are re-establishing their pecking order again."

"You mean they're fighting for dominance over each other?" I asked.

"Right. And the ones who obtain a higher rank in the pecking order feel superior to the ones below. In many species of animals we can see the power struggle of jockeying for position in the herd. It is another part of the survival mechanism we talked about."

"Does this have something to do with why people have such a hard time getting along?" I asked. "Does it have anything to do with me?"

"Yes, Adam. It has to do with all of us. In its meanest and crudest form, this takes the shape of deep, ugly prejudice and justification for people treating other people as less than human. In its more subtle form, jockeying for position in life can be seen in the arrogance of how we put others down or finds fault in others. When we are doing this, it is a clear indication that our mind is dominant."

"So our heart has no interest in putting people down or judging them?" I asked.

"Exactly, and not only that, the heart does not know how," Grandfather chuckled.

"Yeah, but there are times when people are out of line in their behavior, and if your heart does not judge or see it, you can end up being a sucker," I said.

"Adam, I did not say that you should not realize when someone is trying to take advantage of you or put you on a step below them. But if you judge them and develop an attitude, then you got yourself pulled into their game. You end up going head to head with them. Where do you think that leads?"

"Well I guess you butt heads like the two goats were doing a while ago." As I said that, we could hear the two goats going at it and we laughed. I told Grandfather that the goats don't think about it, they just clash their heads and try to destroy one another.

"Adam, I had some peacocks that didn't stop until one of them killed the other."

"I expect they were fighting over territory or a female," I suggested.

"Yes, just as humans have been killing one another over territory boundaries for thousands of years."

"And men fighting over women or women fighting over men," I replied. "I bet their heads are dominant?"

"Adam, when the heart and mind are in alignment, people are not capable of engaging in these types of behaviors. If they do, it means they have floated back up to their head and returned to playing some of the games of the ego. Self-righteous attitudes or being controlling in relationships, are other games. When someone assumes a position of being less than someone else, they have slipped into the inadequacy game. However, when in the middle of a head game, people typically don't realize it. They believe their story line."

"Now that I think about it, I guess there have been power struggles going on even among my friends. Like, who gets to be the leader and who ends up following."

"That's right, Adam. If you study your life, you will see you have played both roles. By finding fault in others it allows you to feel more secure in your own position. When you are feeling more-than another you feel superior, or better, than another person. When you feel less-than another you are feeling insecure or inadequate."

"My friends and I sometimes criticize other groups. I guess it makes us feel like we're better than they are. I also remember being in the less-than position. It seems like some people would like to keep you in that position. They act like they're smarter, or better than you are."

"Adam, you will find yourself in a less-than position only if your heart and mind are not in alignment."

"Now I'm bit confused, Gramps. If it's not best to put yourself in a more-than position, and it's also not good to let yourself be in a less-than position, then what position does that leave you?"

"It leaves you," he said, "in a position in which you do not feel the need to judge others at all. You do not attempt to seek your position in life by comparing yourself to others. And you do not feel you must look up to others as being better than you are. This leaves us all in the position of being equal. We are all siblings, and humanity is our family. The core of our heart is guiding us to experience what this really means."

"Equal? I never really thought of it that way. It sure takes the pressure off."

"I'm not saying we are not to be respectful of others, Adam. There are people who will serve as your teachers and friends, and they may have more life experience and insight than you do. They may have valuable lessons to share with you. There are others," he continued, "who may insult you, or violate your space, but still, this does not change the fact that on a deeper level their human life is a gift and is every bit as precious as yours. We are all a family. They are your siblings even though they don't recognize that you are their brother. In the core of your heart, you know they are your siblings. But from the perspective of your head, you may view them as your enemies."

"Wow, that's deep, really deep, Grandfather."

"Adam, when our hearts are open we become less and less bothered by idiosyncrasies or differences in people. We begin to experience great joy in relationships. We also become more accepting of our own shortcomings, as well as those of others. We easily forgive and we share from our heart. Open hearts live authentically with love, humbleness and gratitude."

It suddenly became very clear to me how grandfather was so quickly and easily able to forgive me for all my mistakes, even for the shooting incident the previous day.

Chapter Twenty-Four
INNATE HEART WISDOM

Grandfather said he felt like it was a good day to build some new birdhouses, and asked me to go out to the shed and gather together some appropriate pieces of scrap wood while he finished repairing his boots.

He came out a few minutes later. Before I knew it, he had constructed two new birdhouses while I was still trying to figure out which pieces of wood to use.

"Slow down, Gramps, you're way ahead of me."

"This is not a competition, Adam."

"Hey, I understand about the importance of equality and all that, but what's wrong with a little competition?"

"There is a place for healthy competition, Adam. But, too often competition becomes another trap."

"Like a weed in the mind, eh?" I asked, grinning.

"Yes, Adam, very good analogy!   It's a weed with deep roots. So, tell me what you think healthy competition is."

"When you play for fun, I guess, and you're not caught up in whether you win or lose."

"Yes, focus for a minute on what it means if you think you have won or lost."

"Gramps, people will consider themselves either winners or losers. It's a less-than or more-than situation, right?"

"Yes, if you allow it to be. The key is to understand that losing a game does not make you a loser. There will always be others who perform a particular task above, or below, your performance level on that particular task."

"Like sports, music, mechanical ability, or I.Q. tests?" I asked.

"Yes, all of those things."

"My I.Q. isn't all that high."

"Oh, yeah? Who said so, Adam?"

"Well, I took the test at school, and. . ."

"Stop right there, Adam. Who made up the test?"

"I guess it was some guy. I don't know who he is."

"Young man, some guy made up a test and someone decided to call it an I.Q. test. Does a high score on that test mean you are intelligent?"

"I think that's what it's supposed to mean, Gramps."

"What it means is, on that particular performance task, you scored a certain way. Who says this guy has a monopoly on the truth regarding what intelligence is? What if we gave him a test based on your life experience? Who would score higher? Adam, I have known men and women who could not read or write, yet they were great teachers. I know people who would not rank on that I.Q. test, yet they could fix just about anything that was broken, or touch your heart with their sincere humbleness. Just because someone scores high on an intelligence test does not mean they are intelligent when it comes to common sense living and getting along with others. It simply means they scored high on that particular performance task. I probably would not score very high on that test if I took it right now, Adam. Would that make me stupid?"

"No, you seem like you've got your act together, Gramps."

"Why, thank you, Adam," he laughed. "The idea is to have fun in the process of whatever task you are performing. The key is to live a heart-centered life and then you can enjoy to the fullest each moment as it unfolds."

"I am so glad to hear I don't have to prove myself by scoring high on tests, because I hate taking them."

"The true test Adam has to do with the quality of your heart. When we allow our heart to open, we get to utilize the gift of our innate heart wisdom that guides us to make wise choices. It helps us to learn lessons that we were failing to learn when we are stuck in our heads and falling into the same 'old holes'. Our innate heart wisdom helps us to perceive the bigger picture and develop greater clarity about situations and relationships."

"It's really amazing to me that we have that kind of intelligence inside our hearts."

"I agree," Grandfather replied. "It exists because of the connection between our heart and the True Source of Love. The perception of our mind is often very limited. Our innate heart wisdom gives us new perspectives, insights and realizations about things. It is the best way to manage whatever challenges come up in our daily lives."

"So who needs the 10 Commandments if you know how to follow your innate heart wisdom?" I remarked.

"You are right, Adam. If your heart is open, you do not have to be told what not to do, because your heart knows. The heart will cringe with the idea of doing something that goes against innate wisdom. But if the head is dominant, you won't be able to feel your innate heart wisdom response. Then there is a chance that you can figure out a way to justify your actions. Adam, this justification of behaviors is how we have gotten ourselves into trouble in the past. Our head will lead us astray. But our open heart will lead us to a genuine, authentic and content filled life."

Chapter Twenty-Five
HEALTHY BOUNDARIES

I wasn't getting paid much money, though Grandfather wasn't working me as hard as I'd expected. We worked only a couple of days a week, and actually spent most of our time outdoors enjoying nature and talking about a lot of things I'd never really given much thought.

After we hung the new birdhouses we lay on our backs on the hillside above the river, watching huge cirrus clouds pass over. Grandfather pointed out one he thought looked like a Chinese dragon. I thought it looked more like a mermaid.

He asked me if, in the past, I had ever found myself caught up in arguments that left me feeling angry or frustrated.

"Oh, sure. That happens," I replied.

"There is a difference between arguments and disagreements, you know."

"Well, my disagreements often lead to arguments. I've gotten really pissed off at my mother when we have tried to discuss things. We've had some real blow-outs."

"Do you remember those arguments?"

"I remember them like they happened yesterday. I'd get angry because I knew I was right and my mother wouldn't admit she was wrong."

"So, you mean, Adam, that she was not seeing things the way you think is right, or the way you think she 'should' see things. This is the most common reason for conflict in relationships. When you experience friction during a conversation," Grandfather continued, "it is probably because you believe that it is not okay for the other person to disagree with you. You think they are supposed to see the world the way you do. That is a signal to let you know your head is dominant"

"So you're saying when I feel an argument brewing, it's because I'm trying to get the other person to see it my way, and I'm not willing to let their views be different from mine?"

"That's right, Adam. And those are the ingredients for a power struggle. You're seeking an 'I am right and you are wrong' solution. People feel justified in their positions, and the truth is things do look different, depending on your perspective. Accepting differences can lead to greater understanding and this is a gift that our heart offers us. Then you can have a heart to heart communication instead of a head to head battle. By accepting that there are differing views, you become more open to understanding the big picture. It is okay to disagree. How boring the world would be if we were all alike!"

"That makes sense, Gramps. I know a lot of the frustration I've had with people is because they didn't agree with me."

"Acceptance of differences leads to harmony and you can be respectful in your disagreements. It gives people space to be who they are, just as you would like to be given the space to be who you are. How did you feel in the past when someone attempted to take that space away from you?"

"Rebellious."

"And others feel rebellious if you take away their space. So, what will you do, Adam, if someone becomes irritated with you because they want you to agree with them?"

"I will allow them to be entitled to their viewpoint, and I can choose to disagree without arguing."

"Easiest way Adam, is to communicate with an open heart. Some people will attempt to get you to fight back by pushing your buttons. They can tell when they push a button in you because it shows on your face. But if you remain grounded in your heart, often they will change."

"Change?" I asked.

"Yes Adam, their position will soften because you are not adding to the competitive energy.

"Ah, so I stop going head to head with them. But Gramps, now I would be communicating from my heart, but they would still be communicating from their head."

"When you shift from head to heart," Grandfather said, "you are no longer playing the same role or acting the same way. You will be amazed at how this will change your relationships for the positive."

"I have to focus on not getting pulled into the drama because that is what happens to me."

"If you shift to feeling your heart, you won't get pulled into the drama. You can also suggest discussing the matter at another time, when emotions are not so flared. The key, Adam, is for your heart to realize that it is okay for people to be different and they do not have to conform to how you think they should think and act. People will notice this and appreciate your acceptance of their differences. It is a sign of maturity and healthy boundaries. "

"I'm not sure I know what you mean by boundaries."

"Boundaries are the quality of interpersonal space we create with a person or circumstance at any given time."

"Oh, they are not fixed boundaries then," I said.

"No, they change from moment to moment and are based on the type and quality of interaction we are having. There are two extremes of unhealthy boundaries: enmeshed boundaries and disengaged boundaries. In the middle of the two extremes is where one establishes healthy boundaries. You will find yourself being pulled toward enmeshment or disengagement in relationships. The key is to monitor your own reactions."

"How can you be sure which way you are being pulled?"

"Adam, have you ever had a phone call, and as soon as you heard the person's voice you felt a knot forming in your gut?"

"Sure. There are a few people who make me feel that way."

"What? Make you feel that way? Are you telling me you are a victim and people toss your feelings around like a horseshoe?" he chuckled.

"Okay. I guess I should say I feel that way when I allow my buttons to get pushed because I'm stuck in my head."

"Yes Adam, this is one type of enmeshment. Your energy field becomes entangled with another's and you lose your sense of personal identity. Even if people attempt to trespass in your space, you do not have to let them in. Every person is responsible for living their own life and bearing the consequences of their behavior. Have heart-felt care for others, but do not lose your space in their space."

"Do you do that naturally when you are in your heart?" I asked.

"Yes you do."

"Then disengaged boundaries must be the opposite", I exclaimed. "You disconnect from the situation."

"Yes. While enmeshment is like a hot type of response, disengagement is a cold response."

"I think I've done that. It's like I shut myself off from the world or another person. One day my boundaries with my mother were enmeshed. Every little thing she did or said pissed me off. The next day I disengaged, and when she spoke to me, I nodded and said 'uh huh,' but didn't hear a word she said."

"Why do you think people develop disengaged boundaries, Adam?"

"Probably because they feel overloaded or hurt, and disconnecting is their defense. They do not realize their head is in charge and causing distress."

"Right. And people who adopt this as a relationship style can feel isolated and lonely. When our boundaries are healthy, we are neither disconnected nor overwhelmed. When our boundaries are healthy," Grandfather continued, "we are respectful of other people's space. We do not view them as less-than or more-than we are, regardless of their behavior. We do not get overdrawn into their drama or their dance, but we do not disconnect either."

"I know now how I've been creating friction in my relationships," I said. "I'll have to work at recognizing boundaries, though."

"Easiest way Adam, is to enjoy the true heart feelings. This allows your heart to remain open, and you will naturally and effortlessly maintain healthy boundaries."

"Accepting differences would help maintain harmony in relationships," I said. "No one is better-than or less-than."

"I could not have said it better myself, Adam. I so much enjoy being your brother rather than your grandfather. Remember, we are all siblings."

Chapter Twenty-Six
THE GREATEST CHOICE

We went for a long walk early one morning and stopped in a field full of colorful wildflowers surrounded by dense forest. In the center of the field was a huge oak tree. We leaned against the trunk and looked out across the field.

I saw a hummingbird darting about among the wildflowers, then stopping in mid-air, its wings were just a blur. I saw a spider spinning a web and was amazed at the complex geometric pattern. A squirrel balanced on a small limb. A butterfly gracefully landed on a wildflower.

"Adam, can you feel that the trees reach to the sun and the sun reaches to the trees? The clouds have a relationship with the wind, just as the birds have a relationship with the sky. Do you see a common denominator?"

"The common denominator I see is a natural intelligence."

"What do you mean by intelligence, Adam?"

"Well, how could a little bird fly south across oceans and mountain ranges and back again to the same nest unless nature was intelligent?"

"Yes, it is truly profound Adam. Instinct is a part of the Gift of Love. It is beyond mental comprehension to grasp life's intelligent design. The earth and other planets in our solar system know their paths around the sun. Can you feel the magic of it all? Yet most people take things for granted. From the perspective of our heart, life is a profoundly awe inspiring experience."

"I can see it, but I'm not sure how much I feel it."

"Guess what, Adam? You are part of that magic. That magic moves in you. It moves in your blood and the core of your heart is directly connected to the Source of your being. How is it your hair knows to grow back the same color and your fingernails grow back when you cut them? The intelligence you see in the beauty of nature expresses itself through you as well. But, do you know what it is that makes you unique in comparison to the rest of nature?"

"No, I don't."

"What will that sparrow be tomorrow, Adam?"

"A sparrow."

"And what will that sparrow be next year?"

"A sparrow."

"How about ten years from now?"

"It'll probably be dead, Gramps."

"That's right, Adam. Could it have changed its mind and been something other than a sparrow?"

"No. Once it's born a sparrow, it lives and dies a sparrow."

"Adam, how are you different from that sparrow?"

"I have more choices?" I guessed.

"Yes, you have choices. You can learn and grow, and become more than you have been. You can develop insight and allow your heart to open in ways you have yet to imagine. You can choose to embrace your life as an exciting journey, or you can take it for granted and sleep through the ride. Your ability to choose is what creates your uniqueness and guides your experience. Value the gift of choice, for it is the treasure that leads to your destiny. Of all choices, what do you feel is the greatest choice we can make?"

"I feel it's to choose to live a heart-centered life instead of living stuck in our head."

Grandfather smiled and let out a big, "yeah." We picked some wildflowers to take back to the cabin. I put them in a vase on the kitchen table. After lunch Grandfather handed me a small box with a ribbon on it. He said it was to express his appreciation for the work I had done. I opened the box and stared, in shock, at what was inside. It was the arrowhead from his collection that I had taken and then returned.

"I felt it would make a nice necklace, Adam," he said, looking intently into my eyes.

I was speechless. He fixed a cord to the arrowhead and put it around my neck. Tears beaded up in my eyes. How do these coincidences keep happening? I thought about what he had told me under the oak tree in the field of wildflowers: Value the gift of choice, for it is the treasure that leads to your destiny.

It was wonderful to know that I always have choices. The holes I've fallen in were the result of my faulty choices. Wow, I was so glad I had chosen to put the arrowhead back.

Chapter Twenty-Seven
BEING IN TUNE

Later that afternoon Grandfather said he was going across the river to check on a stand of bamboo he had planted last year. We had to cross the river by walking on a fallen tree resting several feet above the water. Grandfather skipped across, while I cautiously inched along a half step at a time.

Grandfather was pleased to find the bamboo had nearly doubled in size. He offered to show me how to make a bamboo flute. He looked over each stalk before choosing one, and then gave thanks to the bamboo before he cut it.

We sat down while he carved and filed the bamboo to create a flute. When he had finished he played a few scales, and then surprised me by bursting into a very rhythmic and high-spirited melody. I applauded him afterward. Then he played another song that was obviously out of tune.

"What did you think of that song, Adam?" he asked.

"To be honest with you, I didn't like it as well as the first one because it sounded out of tune."

"How did you know?"

"Well, I just knew, I guess."

"What do you mean, you just knew?"

"Not sure Gramps. I just knew."

"Adam, I believe you were able to observe that my second song was out of tune and out of rhythm because you have a reference point."

"What do you mean?"

"You compared it to what you think an 'in tune' song sounds like. The 'in tune' song is your reference point." Grandfather handed the flute to me. I tried playing a few notes.

"I guess people can be in tune or out of tune, too, eh?" I said.

"That's true, Adam. What do you think it means to be in tune?"

I immediately thought back to our conversations about being heart centered.

"Being out of tune means you are off center, right?" I asked. "It's like getting caught up in your own soap opera or dance. You feel agitated or frustrated and your head is in charge."

"Yes. It is like being in the soup and not even knowing you are being cooked! Each of us has the potential to get out of the soup, Adam, but unfortunately many people do not even know when they are in it."

"Are you talking about me?" I asked.

"It is your personal responsibility to figure that out, Adam. If a person has not developed the peaceful, calm reference point of the heart, then they may not recognize when they are out of tune."

"It seems like sometimes I have no control over myself. I've probably been a real jerk and didn't even know it."

"I have had my share of putting my foot in my mouth, too, Adam. The point is, it is crucial that we develop an internal reference point to minimize the mistakes we make through our words, thoughts and actions."

"How do you do that?"

"You practice being in tune. You learn what it feels like to live with an open heart. You have to learn to do this, even when your eyes are open. It's a joy to learn to live and operate from that space.

"And, just as important," Grandfather continued, "you practice recognizing when you are out of tune. When you realize you are functioning from the limitations of mind dominance, you begin to tune in to your heart by feeling your true heart feelings. Without this commitment, you cannot learn to live a life of harmony. Oh, and remember Adam, being in your heart does not mean that you ignore your head. When the heart is dominant, your brain becomes your friend that works in harmony with your heart. This relationship serves your highest good and allows you to make wise choices."

"It seems to me, Gramps, you're saying that learning to recognize when we are out of tune gives us an alert signal that it is time to get back into our heart."

"Yes, it can, Adam, so your heart and mind can come back into alignment."

Chapter Twenty-Eight
THEATER OF LIFE

Although I had been at LotusHeart cabin for only a few weeks, those weeks felt like months. It seemed like so much had happened. I could not make sense of it all and my head was spinning. I kept thinking it was my head that was real, and not my heart. Sometimes everything made perfect sense and other times I doubted Gramps and what he was telling me." If I let my heart take over, some people may take advantage of me. And what about me and my desires and my needs? If I don't look after me, no one will," I thought.

Even though I enjoyed the peacefulness and the beauty of the mountains, I also found myself wondering about my friends back at home. It seemed like I was living in a make believe world that was so different than the world I knew before. A war could have broken out and we wouldn't have known about it. Grandfather had a radio but seldom turned it on.

We had worked for three days building a new shed that was now finished. I thought it was a good time to ask for a little break. It was late afternoon on a Saturday, and I was feeling especially restless.

"Hey, Gramps, if it's okay with you, I thought I'd go home tonight and come back in a few days."

"Sounds like something is cooking, Adam. Anything you would like to talk about?"

"Oh, I don't know. I just feel like I need a break. I want to see my friends."

"Your leaving is not what concerns me. I feel you are running away from yourself. Or should I say, you are running away from your heart."

"What do you mean, Gramps?" I started feeling impatient.

"You came here this summer to work, and I do not think you expected to be going through these changes in your life. You have learned a lot in a short period of time and that can be scary. Your old world has been shaken up."

"I'm not scared. I just want to get out of here for a few days."

"You are not the same young man who came here. Your model of reality is in the process of change. I wonder if letting go of your old stuff is feeling like a challenge."

"I'm getting tired of all this heart stuff, Gramps. Living with you is intense. I just need a break. Will you let me go?"

"Of course, Adam. This is not a prison. And if you decide you would rather not come back, that's your choice."

"I'll be back," I smiled, feeling relieved. "I want to come back. I kind of like it out here."

I took my backpack and walked down the trail and followed the dirt road out to the main highway to hitch a ride. Within just a few minutes a car stopped. As I approached the car I saw three guys about my age inside, all drinking beer and there was an open bottle of booze. They also looked really stoned. My heart raised a big red flag before my eyes: "Do not get in the car." I thought maybe I was just being paranoid. My head was not interested in what my heart had to say. They seemed friendly, just out having fun and getting a little rowdy. I really didn't feel like waiting for another ride. One of them swung open the back door and I climbed in.

I noticed a number of empty beer cans on the floor. One of the guys offered me a beer. I started to refuse it but changed my mind. I was actually quite thirsty from the walk. It tasted great. We were cruising down the road with the stereo turned up and everyone singing along. I started feeling like my old self again.

We hadn't gone very far when we passed by a highway patrol car parked by the side of the road, partially concealed by shrubs. I glanced at the speedometer. We were speeding. The guy who was driving saw the worried look on my face. He laughed and sped up even more. Evidently no one else had seen the patrol car.

"Hey, man, there's a cop!" I shouted to be heard over the blaring music. It was too late. The police were already coming up behind us.

"Aw, shit! Not again," the driver moaned and shut the music off. "Hey, I was just goofing around with you," he said to me. The other two guys were trying frantically to shove all the empty beer cans under the seats.

The patrol car's flashing lights came on, and we pulled onto the shoulder of the road and stopped. The guys were all cussing about their bad luck. I felt numb. All I had wanted was to go home for a few days.

When the officers began to ask questions, the driver, trying to be funny, responded with some sarcastic remarks, and that was the end of my trip home. We were all handcuffed and taken to the local jail. I explained my situation to the police. I told them how to get in touch with Grandfather Sage, and that he would come and get me.

A few hours later Grandfather showed up. He was brought to our cell and when he was asked if he knew any of us, he looked at me and said, "Yes, I recognize that guy in the corner of the cell who looks really stuck in his head." He turned and walked out.

I was furious. The rest of the guys were already passed out, but I didn't sleep a wink all night.

In the morning Grandfather returned. He spoke with the police chief in private. I was released.

"Why did you make me spend the night in jail?" I demanded. "I can't believe you would do that to me! Did you get a kick out of it? I'm pissed at you!"

He made no apologies. He didn't even respond to my accusations. He was as cheerful as if nothing had happened. He stopped the truck at a small market and said, "I will be right back." He returned a few minutes later with a large bag of popcorn.

"For the theater of life, Adam," he grinned. We ate the popcorn on the way back to the cabin.

Chapter Twenty-Nine
WHO AM I

That afternoon back at the cabin Grandfather was shucking corn he'd had left over from the previous year's harvest that he intended to cut from the cobs and feed to the squirrels. I sat at the kitchen table watching him, too exhausted to do anything from lack of sleep. I was depressed and felt foolish for having gotten myself into another jam. I hadn't even made it to the next county without getting into trouble.

"Do not wallow in your guilt, Adam. Just figure out what really happened and move on."

"Before I got in the car with those guys a big red flag went up, but I ignored it."

"Sounds to me like you sabotaged yourself again. You chose your head over the wisdom of your heart. Those messages you picked up from your environment and your father are your core beliefs that keep playing over and over."

"But my father is dead. He can't put me down anymore."

"Adam, you told me that your father treated you like you were not good enough."

"Yeah. Whatever I did, it wasn't good enough."

"Those messages still exist in your unconscious and affect your present experience. Adam, he was just mirroring to you his own inadequacy. Your father is no longer physically present, but his messages live on in the form of your underlying belief that you will never amount to anything." Grandfather set aside the corn he was shucking and sat down across from me at the kitchen table.

"Isn't it interesting that you keep finding yourself in situations which confirm this?" he asked.

"It does seem to keep happening. I just wind up in the wrong place at the wrong time."

"Don't you get it, Adam? You do not just end up there by accident. Your underlying beliefs generate an actual vibration that is constantly emanating from you. A part of you attracts these circumstances and allows you to engage in the drama. This is happening when you are stuck in your head. When you are in your heart, you are not capable of creating this sabotage.

"Some people cannot handle it when things are going smoothly," he continued.

"They look for arguments, or create a crisis. Then a part of them can say, 'Yeah, this is more like it. Now it feels normal.' They may not be aware they are being governed this way, but they are. They grew up in crisis, and as an adult they seek out crisis because that is what feels normal to them. Others continue to re-create patterns of worry, dissatisfaction, fear, loneliness, arrogance, insecurity, greed or other non-constructive patterns."

I suddenly realized what he was trying to tell me all along. Shaking my head, I let out a big sigh. It made so much sense.

"Life is a process, Adam, in which we learn to wake up from the trances of every-day life and learn to live a heart-centered life. Emotional trances interfere with our ability to live in harmony. And you re-create trances when you allow your head to be your home."

"You've said peace, joy and love is the true nature of our heart?"

"Yes, Adam. And emotional patterns that take us out of balance are reflections of these trances we create in our heads."

"Are you saying it's not good to have emotions?" I asked.

"Remember there is a difference between emotions and true heart feelings. Many emotions are patterns replaying themselves without your permission. They are stuck, or unfinished, parts of you which resurface as they are triggered. When you are living in your head, you also create excuses, rationalizations and justifications for why you have a right to have these strong emotions.

"As I shared with you before, true heart feelings are the natural expressions of your heart. You are not the creator or originator of the peace, calm, joy and love from your heart. You simply experience the beauty of your heart that is present from the direct connection of your heart with the True Source of Unconditional Love. Many people live their lives moving from one emotional trance into another. One moment they might feel insecure. The next moment they may be judgmental. Another moment they may be embellishing their sense of superiority. They are confused because they think their emotional creations are absolute reality."

"How can you wake up from the trance when you don't even know you're in it?" I asked.

"That is a process which develops over time. First, we learn to recognize the trances of our everyday life. You have to know to recognize when you are in your head and 'out of tune'. We discussed this before, Adam. First, we choose to learn to have fun observing ourselves in these trances. Then we learn to wake up from the garbage we create in our heads. Feeling the true heart feelings so that your heart can open bigger is of course the key. But please don't be too hard on yourself when you catch yourself off center. Being hard on ourselves is another type of trance that keeps us locked in our head."

"I know that one," I said.

"Have the courage to examine you. It can be fun discovering who you are not, and then you can discover who you are. These trances are not who you really are."

"Then who am I?"

"Adam, when you learn to live a heart-centered life, the limited aspects of our self falls away, and the true us emerges. Through our heart's connection with the True Source of Unconditional Love, we can experience who we really are."

Chapter Thirty
COLORED LENSES

After splitting and stacking some firewood following dinner that night, I collapsed under a tree to relax for a while before going to bed. Grandfather came out of the cabin and lay down on the grass.

"By the way, Adam, I forgot to tell you there are rattlesnakes and copperheads in these woods. Be careful."

"I don't like snakes. Have you ever been bitten, Gramps?"

"Only a few times. I almost died once, but guess it was not my time to go." He smiled, and I wasn't sure if he was joking.

He got up and went back into the cabin and returned a few minutes later with a basket of fruit. I was about to bite into an apple when suddenly Grandfather's eyes opened wide and he shouted, "Look out!" He reached to my side and picked up a two-foot long snake and began wrestling with it.

I sprang to my feet and ran thirty feet across the yard before looking back. Grandfather was rolling in laughter. Then I realized it wasn't a snake but a piece of rubber hose he'd brought from the cabin concealed among the fruit.

"That was mean, Gramps," I said. "Why did you yell 'look out for that snake?'"

"I didn't, Adam. I simply said 'look out.' Your mind created the rest of the story. You saw what you feared. Your fear was projected into the world and that piece of garden hose became your fear."

"But it looked real. I could have sworn that hose was a snake."

"Adam, when I was a youth I was very self-conscious. One day a group of people was staring at me. I was convinced they were talking about me until realizing they were actually looking at someone standing behind me."

"You know, Gramps, the same thing happened to me once. I was in a large stadium watching a football game. When one of the teams went into a huddle, I just knew they were talking about me."

"Are you serious, Adam?"

"Gotcha, Gramps!"

He smiled. "Well, I am glad to hear you are kidding."

"I know what you're talking about, though," I said. "What you believe inside affects what you perceive on the outside. If you're gloomy inside, life can look gloomy on a sunny day."

"Well said, my brother. Yes, and if you are bright on the inside, life will feel and look bright even on a gloomy day."

"I once had a pair of glasses that had a blue tint to them. I wore them all day. After a while I forgot I was wearing them and wondered why everything looked so bluish. Later, when I took the lenses off everything looked very different."

"So what's the moral of your story, Adam?"

"We don't always see as clearly as we think we're seeing. We think we're seeing and experiencing the world as it is, but in reality we're only seeing the world as it's reflected through the colored lenses of our mind."

"Yes, Adam. These lenses can be made up of many different colors, thicknesses and textures, which are the unresolved wounds we carry around with us – hurts, rejections, fears and resentments that have not healed. Even though you may not realize it, you have not completely forgiven yourself or others. Limiting beliefs and conditioning color our perceptions. Many people go through an entire lifetime without questioning, and with little change in how they view reality."

"So my experience with that hose was one of those colored lenses," I said.

"It sure was, Adam," Grandfather chuckled.

"I went into a full-blown survival mechanism fight/flight response."

"Isn't it wonderful that you got to confront your fear face to face, Adam? You know if you would have been in your heart, you would have seen right through the hose and you would not have gotten spooked."

"Very funny Gramps. And by the way, how am I going to get to deal with all my resentments, hurts, and anger?"

"Are you ready Adam?"

"Well, I didn't say that. I was just wondering."

Chapter Thirty-One
HEARTFULL VS MINDFULL

That evening we took sleeping bags and hiked to the top of the highest ridge in the area. It was the day of summer solstice and Grandfather wanted to celebrate by spending the night under the stars. There was a magnificent view of the foothills all around us. The sun was setting. We sat on a rock outcropping facing west and watched the changing colors in the sky and the colorful cloud formations passing over.

"Did you ever sit on a bench and watch people go by?" Grandfather asked.

"Yes, I have," I replied. "It seemed like everyone was in a world of their own, as if they were living their own personal soap operas. I could see it on their faces as they walked by."

"I have some interesting news for you, Adam. You are living your own soap opera, too. If we took a video of your mind from the time you woke up until the time you went to sleep, what would we find?"

"We'd probably find that I waste a lot of time," I said.

"Waste time on what?"

"Trivial things, I guess, stuff that really doesn't matter. I'm always doing, or going, or thinking."

"Where do those mental activities take you, Adam?"

"Into either the past or the future, I guess."

"Yes. The mind gets caught up in lots of thoughts, and there is a lack of awareness where much personal drama gets created. The mind often runs on automatic pilot. Thoughts come and go without your permission."

"That happens to me all the time. I'll tell myself I don't want to think about something anymore, but it keeps coming back to me."

"Do you give it permission to come back?"

"No."

"Then those thought patterns are on automatic pilot. Those thoughts are thinking you."

"Grandfather, I saw a book on your shelf in the living room, and it talked about 'mindfulness'. I skimmed through it."

"That is an old book of mine. I used to regularly practice mindfulness and found it to have value as a stress management tool. I do not practice mindfulness anymore."

"If it had value, why did you stop?"

"It had value at the time, but then it became a hindrance once I realized that our heart is the key to happiness and a fulfilled life."

"You will have to explain that one to me."

"Adam, how about I support you in figuring out the answer for yourself? Then it will be more meaningful to you."

"Go for it."

"Close your eyes Adam and be mindful of everything going on. If you have a thought be aware that you are having a thought. What ever is present, be aware of that. Now tell me what that experience is like."

"I feel like an observer in my mind, witnessing whatever is going on."

"Yes Adam, you are correct. Mindfulness can be a wonderful stress management tool, because rather than being caught up in the drama of your mind, you become aware of what you have created in your head. The act of observation shifts the experience. I learned to separate myself from my emotional reactivity so that I could observe it rather than be it. Experiencing the space between my thoughts and the space between my breaths was a valuable stepping stone. Mindfulness allowed me to heighten my sense awareness so that I could taste a raisin like I never have before or hear the sounds of nature as if I was hearing them for the first time.

"So I don't understand why you stopped doing this? It seems really helpful."

"Close your eyes Adam, relax and smile to your heart. Enjoy the true heart feelings and how the gentle joy is radiating from your heart. Enjoy more, and keep feeling the true heart feelings. Realize this beauty exists from the connection of your heart with the True Source of Unconditional Love. Feel how much of you is enjoying, and how much of you is in your head observing your heart? Now allow yourself to be even more mindful and completely observe and be aware of the nice feelings in your heart. What happened?"

"That was interesting. I could feel that the true heart feelings lessened and it did not feel as good when I became more mindful. More of me was observing and less was feeling the beauty of the heart."

"Yes, Adam. Wonderful insight."

"When you asked me to observe more, I noticed that the radiance of the true heart feelings decreased."

"Now you understand why I stopped my mindfulness practice. It kept me separated from my heart. It was like a great celebration was going on in my heart, and the bigger part of me was outside in the cold peaking through the window," Grandfather chuckled, "Although I am grateful for the lessons mindfulness taught me and how it served as a stepping stone to my experience of being heart centered."

"How do you get all of you to enjoy the celebration of your heart?" I asked.

"My heart is so happy to feel your sincere question. I shared with you that following the true heart feelings will open your heart more. The reason you observe, is because you do not fully trust your heart and you do not yet trust the connection between your heart and the True Source of Unconditional Love. Mindfulness can be limited in its ability to lead you into the depths of your heart. The reason is that when you are mindful, you typically observe your heart from a distance. My experience with mindfulness is that it eventually leads to a plateau and you just learn to hang out in that space. But the intimate quality of heartfullness just keeps getting sweeter and more joyful, even when you think there is no way it can ever get better than this. The innate longing within us to feel profoundly safe and unconditionally loved is fulfilled through the doorway of our heart."

"Wow Grandfather, I am so glad you showed me the way of the heart. I am ready to enjoy more. Enough of these mental head trips I keep creating."

"Adam, I look forward to your future enjoyments."

Chapter Thirty-Two
LETTING THE LOVE WORK

I gathered some sticks and we built a small camp-fire when the last light of dusk had gone.

"Adam, I am going to hang out and enjoy the Gift of Unconditional Love and you are welcome to join me."

"I'd like to join you, but I don't know how. I can feel my heart a bit, but not like you do."

"Well then, Adam, it is time for a heart adjustment. Just keep feeling the true heart feelings so that the connection between your heart and the True Source of Unconditional Love can grow. Keep relaxing while enjoying and let the Unconditional Love remove the blockages in your heart and replace them with love and gratefulness."

As grandfather sat in silence, I could feel something opening up in the center of my chest as blockages were being removed. I could feel my non-physical heart was expanding and opening bigger. It was such a beautiful feeling to experience my heart opening more.

We practiced together, and I was able to feel how easy it is to enjoy my heart. I did not have to do anything to get there except to enjoy the true heart feelings. The more I enjoyed, the more I could feel the boundaries of my heart expanding, and the peace and joy kept growing.

We hung out until the fire died down and a few coals remained. The full moon was beginning to rise.

"Adam, I enjoyed sharing that heart space with you. It is a way in which we communicate deeply without words. Now I would like to communicate with words."

"What would you like to talk about?" I asked.

"What did you notice, Adam, when you were enjoying a deeper connection with your heart?"

"When I was enjoying, it was like eating an ice-cream cone, one lick at a time. It felt so easy and wonderful. Time seemed to stand still. There was no past or future. I could feel the boundary of my heart opening and expanding bigger and bigger."

"Fantastic, I am so happy to hear that."

"As I kept following and feeling the beautiful feelings, a pressure deep inside surfaced and it felt uncomfortable."

"Adam, those are blockages surfacing that have come up to be cleansed."

"What kind of blockages?" I asked.

"It does not matter. Blockages come in so many shapes and forms. For example, they can be related to resentments, anger, hurt, disappointments, rejection, and un-forgiveness towards ourselves and others. We don't have to understand their origin."

"Grandfather, if we don't understand where the blockages come from, how can we get rid of them?"

"You are not the one responsible for getting rid of them."

"That makes no sense," I said.

"You are right. It makes no sense to your head. But to your heart, it makes total sense. Only the True Source of Unconditional Love can easily remove the blockages in the inner layers of your heart. When you enjoy and let Unconditional Love work, the blockages are easily removed. The Gift of Unconditional Love always wants to give us the best. Only we separate ourselves because we have chosen to live in our head. The Source of Love is always willing to help us by removing everything that is not for our highest good."

"I have trouble believing it can be that easy."

"I was not able to believe it either, until experiencing how the True Source of Love never wants us to live in separation. It is our destiny for our heart to be free from all blockages so that we can live a heart-centered life, and allow the gentleness of Love to radiate.

"Would you like to know the hard part Adam?"

"Yes, I would."

"Not holding onto your stuff on the way out. When the Source of Love cleanses the blockages, you have to be careful not to cling to it or the released blockage will get stuck."

"So you are saying I've got to stay relaxed?" I asked.

"Yes, Adam, relaxed, smiling and feeling the true heart feelings. Then the True Source of Love can remove the blockages that do not serve us. Instead of resisting and staying head strong, we accept the Gift of Unconditional Love."

Chapter Thirty-Three
AWARENESS

Grandfather went into town one morning to get some building materials. I stayed behind. A huge, old oak tree in the yard that had a strong branch up high seemed perfect for hanging a swing. I decided to put it up and surprise Grandfather when he returned.

I found everything needed in the shed and climbed up the tree to fasten the ropes. I sanded a scrap of oak I'd found for the seat and applied a dark stain that brought out the beauty of the wood grain.

After going down to the river for a swim, I sat on the bank, and enjoyed dissolving into the true heart feelings as I began to feel more wonderful feelings than I had ever imagined I could feel. I was finding it easier to let the gentleness of Love remove my doubt, anger, fear, insecurity and judgments that so commonly surfaced to my mind and replace them with love and gratefulness. But very deep down I could sense there were also hidden layers of different emotions like anger, arrogance, greed, pride, jealousy, guilt and shame. I could feel un-forgiveness toward myself and resentments I still carried toward others. I felt deeper peace and could tell that these blockages were softening. But I also felt I needed to keep a wall up or else I might cease to exist.

Grandfather returned a couple of hours later. When I got back to the LotusHeart Cabin he was swinging, and singing, "Love Is All You Need." I sat down and listened. His voice did not sound very good, but his singing sure did make my heart feel happy.

He was very pleased with the swing and complimented me on my craftsmanship. He asked me to take off my arrowhead necklace for a moment. I handed it to him, and he began swinging it back and forth like a pendulum. He let the pendulum come to a rest and explained that this represents the center, where the gentleness of Love can shine through without obstruction.

When the pendulum swings, it swings away from the center. It may swing into the caution zone, or even further, into the danger zone. Our heart zone is the range in which our pendulum swings from left to right while we are able to remain with an open heart, calm and peaceful.

"What's the caution zone?" I asked.

"That is where you get so off center you begin to feel or act imbalanced. Know what I mean?"

"I think so. My old tendency was to act cool even though I was feeling insecure. I worried about things that couldn't be changed, and I'd get irritable when things didn't go the way I thought they should."

"Yes, Adam. Those are examples of the caution zone, maybe even the danger zone. In the caution zone the trance is not so deep. You are able to step back and recognize that you are no longer in the heart zone. You can then choose to return to the heart zone by letting the gentleness of Love bring you there. It's like stepping out of a trance. It is a lot easier to catch yourself off track and return to the heart zone when you are in the caution zone."

"Because you're not so far off from center?"

"Exactly. When you move way off center it is a bigger challenge to get yourself out of that denser trance. You're more stuck in your head and don't realize it. This is why awareness is important. Awareness allows us to monitor the pendulum swing. And the good news is that the Gift of Love is always present to bring us deeper into the safety and joy of our heart."

"I guess if you lack awareness you fall into the hole again. Same old game and same old trance."

"Yes, Adam. Our home-joy, not home-work, is to learn how to function and live in the heart zone. Practice will allow you to notice when you are in the caution or danger zones. You will learn to let Unconditional Love bring you back into the calm, peace and joy of the heart zone."

"Is that all there is to it?"

"Why complicate something that is so simple? At any given moment the True Source of Unconditional Love is present. If you are being insecure, you want to recognize your insecurity. If you are being self-centered, you want to know it. If you are worrying, acknowledge you are worrying. If your mind is racing, realize you are ahead of yourself. Be present to whatever trance of your mind you may be in. Be grateful that this pattern is not who you truly are. Then let the Source of Love remove your emotional preoccupation or judgmental thoughts and replace them with love and gratefulness. Just relax, smile, come back to feeling the true heart feelings and let it happen."

"It's like observing myself in my own movie theater."

"Yes, Adam. And guess what?" he laughed. "You have the best seat in the house! If you experience yourself acting like you are better than someone else, you get to realize your judgmental attitude. You discover that you are in a trance of superiority. If you are acting or feeling like you are not good enough, you get to witness your feelings of inadequacy. Then it is time to return to the heart zone. This is where the Source of Love wants you to be, not stuck in your head or emotional reactivity. Your dominant mind is where you suffer from separation while failing to realize how disconnected you are at that time."

"So our awareness teaches us to recognize our trances," I said.

"Yes, it does. At any given moment all you have to do is ask, 'What am I doing, thinking or feeling at this moment?' Just remain present," he said. "Don't worry about being pulled out of the heart zone, because that will happen again and again. Just don't stay gone too long," Grandfather chuckled. "We are learning to rely on the True Source of Love to help us so that we can live a heart-centered life enjoying the gentleness of Love and gratefulness"

"Sounds like when I am in the trances I create in my mind, I am sleeping. When I return to the heart zone, I awaken."

"Yes Adam, for example you wake up from the trance of inadequacy or superiority, greed or worry. Before you became aware, Adam, those patterns were occurring without your permission."

"This all makes so much sense, Grandfather. Why don't they teach us this in school?"

"Let's just say you are learning them in earth school, the great classroom of life!"

Chapter Thirty-Four
TRAPPED BETWEEN TWO WORLDS

In the early morning, we walked up to the mountain ridge to enjoy the sunrise. We meditated together and in silence. I was beginning to feel I was not looking at life through the same eyes. The way I felt and responded to things seemed so different. The deep peace and feeling of being more connected to life was a new experience for me. It was so beautiful. I could feel my heart becoming more grateful for all that I had received. Something became very free inside the center of my body. I could feel a sweet opening above my head that flowed through my body and connected deep to the earth.

"Grandfather, this feels like nothing I have ever felt before. How come I feel this opening inside of my body? It feels so free."

"Adam, I explained that when we open our heart, we are opening our non-physical heart. Likewise, we have major energy centers that run along the core energy channel in the center of your body. Now you have a deeper connection to the earth and the flow of Love entering your body through the crown center is flowing more freely. The connection between the core of your heart and the True Source of Love is growing."

"I can feel the softness of love flowing through the crown down to the core of my heart and gently radiating without any effort on my part."

"Wonderful, Adam. Now you will be able to learn how to enjoy the gentle sublime quality of Unconditional Love. Even more, and most importantly, how to be an instrument and let your heart radiate what has been unconditionally given."

"Now that's cool. Gramps, I am getting hungry, how about you?"

After breakfast I was spreading some mulch in the garden when Grandfather came out and told me he thought it would be a good idea to give my mother a call to see how she was doing. I told him I'd call her that evening. He strongly suggested I call right away. I went down to the general store to use the telephone.

My aunt answered the phone. She was packing a bag of clothes to take to my mother, who was in the hospital. Earlier in the day a bicyclist had run into Mom as she was crossing the street and knocked her over backward. She had suffered a broken leg and hit her head on the concrete.

Grandfather said I could borrow his truck. I packed a few things and left immediately. Mom was released from the hospital the next day and was able to get around somewhat with crutches.

For two days I helped Mom with food preparation and chores. My aunt, who lived nearby, was able to help as well, so Mom insisted I return to LotusHeart Cabin and finish my summer work with Grandfather Sage. She was concerned I would get caught up in an old rut with my friends. I agreed and planned to leave early the following day.

Later, while I was doing some grocery shopping for Mom, I ran into one of my friends. When I returned home, four other guys called, insisting we go out and party that night. I decided to go meet them.

I met them at the park where we used to hang out. They brought a couple cases of beer, and we began the old routine. While sipping on a beer, some of the other guys chugged down four cans. I felt torn between two worlds. One part of me just wanted to be one of the guys and the other wanted to follow my heart. I reflected back on how much fun I thought we had together getting drunk, being silly, and acting stupid without a care in the world. To try to fit in, I grabbed another can of beer and chugged it half way down. Then I stopped in my tracks as I felt my heart saying, "Is this the path you want to choose in this moment?" It felt that the innate wisdom of my heart had spoken, and I better listen or else I will do something stupid like I did in the past. I took a moment to relax, smile and naturally feel the true heart feelings. I could feel myself getting back into sync and now had one foot back in the heart zone. I became aware of how my friends interacted and could see how they were caught up in judging and putting others down. This gave them a false sense of superiority. This is what I used to call "fun", and how seductive it felt to think I was better than others. My friends were bragging and seeking to secure a more-than position. I saw how some of them were doing this in response to feeling insecure, a less-than position. Wow, I realized this used to be a very normal mental response for me, and now it felt so strange.

"Hey guys, does it really make you feel better to put everybody down?"

Frank stepped forward and blasted me stating, "Who in the hell do you think you are. What's wrong with you! You used to enjoy this too. Did you fall for a bunch of crap up in the mountains with that old man?"

"Frank, we don't need to feel good by putting others down. We are not a pack of roosters, and thinking you're the head rooster is an illusion and I don't buy into that.

"Hey, lets just deal with it right here," Frank shouted.

Frank's chest was puffed out, his eyes were bulging and his nose was flaring. He thought I was jockeying for his position. At first I could feel my emotions begin to flare. I was so close to cursing him out, I was about to explode. I knew they couldn't understand where I was coming from, so I let it go. It then became clear to me that I was judging and putting them down, just like they were now putting down others. Wow, the mind is so tricky.

I smiled, slapped him on the back, and said, "Come on Frank, relax, I'm just playing around."

I could feel the battle between my heart and head going on and felt pulled in both directions. The conflict of being trapped between two worlds was staring me in the face. I told my friends about the trap of being 'stuck in the head' and how peaceful and calm it is to live from the heart. I wanted to share about my experience of how I changed. Having one foot in their world and one foot in Grandfather's world......I felt trapped between two worlds that did not see eye to eye.

My friends began to get defensive because they thought they knew me and now they were confused about who I was. Not long ago I hung out with these guys on a daily basis, and this was how I thought and acted. Focusing on women, sex, money and partying no longer had the same appeal. I sat in silence.

Frank confronted me again. "What's wrong with you, man?" he demanded. "Have you sold out on us? What has that old guy you're working for done to you? Have you been brainwashed, or what?"

I explained that I used to live my life in a trance so it seemed like I was surrounded by a thick fog, and now I was beginning to awaken from that trance. They had no idea what I was talking about. Attempting to share how we are walking around with colored lenses that color the way we see the world was greeted with rolling eyes. I explained how we are trapped living in our head, and we don't even realize it. I shared how our heart is the key to happiness and a fulfilled life. What we are all searching for is our own heart. They looked at each other, dumbfounded.

I shared that we can learn to live a heart-centered life while enjoying relationships and not getting into 'head trips'. I explained how wonderful it is to have a heart to heart with someone, instead of bumping heads. They could not understand when I told them that I felt like a completely different person, and was much more happy and comfortable with myself.

"Frank we don't have to keep getting our 'buttons pushed' and it is time for us to let go of our excuses or blaming others for why things are not how we want them to be."

After sharing that our heart is not something to fear, because it offers us our greatest gift, I could tell that Frank was really squirming. The attitude of the other guys shifted and they wanted to hear more. Frank was the ring leader, and took charge.

"Let's go get really stoned. The night is young," Frank said. They jumped in Joe's van and wanted me to come along. I could feel my heart cringe just with the idea of going with them. I was sure Joe was intoxicated. I chose to go home instead.

I stared up at the ceiling as I lay in bed feeling trapped between two worlds. I no longer fit into my old world with my friends. They didn't understand me, and I really didn't completely understand Grandfather's world. It seemed as if I had come to a fork in the road, torn between two paths. One path was my old world; the other path, Grandfather's world.

Asking my heart to show me what would happen if I followed the path my friends are on, the path grew darker and darker over time. I asked my heart to show me how my life would be if I chose Grandfather's road. The path felt brighter as time moved forward. Grandfather's road led to freedom and joy. Yet I felt confused because there was still a part of me that felt attracted to my old ways and my old friends.

Chapter Thirty-Five
THE HIGHWAY HOME

After arriving at the LotusHeart cabin early the next afternoon I found Grandfather meditating down by the waterfall. I tried to sneak up behind him. I got within ten feet of him, and he turned around and smiled.

"Did you get lost, Adam?"

"No, I didn't," I said. "It was an easy drive."

"That's good. I knew there was a fork in the road and I am glad you chose the right path." His response took me by surprise.

"Gramps, I don't know how you happen to know these things. I do know you're not as weird as I used to think you were."

"Why, thank you, Adam. You are not quite as weird as you used to seem to me, as well," he chuckled. "Did you find any opportunities to use your innate heart wisdom?"

"Yes. When I was offered the opportunity to ride in the van with my friends, my heart contracted and it was firmly telling me, "don't go". I'm glad I followed my heart and not my head."

"Me too, Adam," grandfather laughed. "Anyway, the fun has just begun."

"What do you mean by that?"

"Now that you have consciously chosen your path, a new level of wonderful experiences await you."

I didn't understand until many weeks later what he meant.

That evening Grandfather gathered sticks from the forested area surrounding the Lotus Heart Cabin and built a special campfire to welcome me back. I told him about my trip home, and what I had observed among my friends. He sat smiling and listening, but didn't say a word. I eventually finished my story and we then enjoyed staring into the fire. Nearly an hour passed before Grandfather broke the silence.

"Adam, you are going through a wonderful growth process, and these adventures are preparing you for the next stage in this process. You have made some very positive changes. Your heart has opened so beautifully. You will begin to attract friends who will nourish you, and likewise, you will nourish them because of your heart's connection to the Source of Love. You have also become more aware of the synchronicities of life."

"Synchronicities?" I asked.

"That means life's events are not occurring merely by chance."

"I'm beginning to feel like life does have an arrangement."

"Yes, my brother, an amazing arrangement beyond our mind's comprehension."

"I think you and I getting together was synchronicity," I said.

"Yes, Adam. This is a gift for both of us. It was not chance that our paths have crossed."

"It's amazing, Gramps! Life is so intelligent, and we are all unconditionally loved....but so many people seem to have blinders on."

"As you are in the process of developing yourself, Adam, you will attract, and be attracted to, friends who will resonate with you."

"You mean we'll be on the same wavelength?" I asked.

"Yes. Birds of a feather do, indeed, flock together. Your vibration is so much different than it was before. A big shift has taken place within you because your heart is now open, and you are not living your life from your head. Now you will attract and seek friends who are on a parallel wavelength. To spend all your time with friends who are not heart centered may feel shallow to you."

"Grandfather, it's no fun hanging around people who keep falling in the same old holes, especially if they're not interested in getting out of them."

"Adam, be careful not to get cocky. You still have your share of holes."

"Give me a break, Gramps. I'm not lost in a better-than attitude trance."

"Just checking, Adam. Its easy to fall into the hole of judgment, because our heads have played that game for so long."

I saw him smile with a twinkle in his eyes in the flickering light of the fire. We sat quietly for a few minutes.

"So, Adam, if you saw a friend falling in the same hole repeatedly, what kind of friend would you be to stand by and let him keep falling without saying anything?"

"Well... It's kind of tricky. It didn't work so well when I tried to help my old friends on my visit home. I did say something, but it didn't go over very well. After that experience, I'd be afraid of rocking the boat. I don't know, Gramps. How can you help friends who are screwing up?"

"The same way you would like to be supported."

"Hmm...Well, I'd like people to listen, and not judge me."

"I understand, Adam. If we allow friends to be imperfect, and we do not condemn them for it, then it creates a safe space."

"I brought a lot of problems with me when I came here. Thank you for putting up with me, Grandfather. Your friendship has helped me incredibly."

"It has been a joy, Adam. Friends can be a good sounding board to help clarify issues for you, especially if you 'heart storm' together."

"You mean instead of brainstorm?" I asked.

"Yes, but you can only heart storm from your heart, not your head", Grandfather chuckled. "Choosing friends who resonate with where you are at sure makes life easier. Close your eyes and let your heart feel this Adam. You are walking your path. The purpose of your journey is to let your heart open more and more so you can live a heart-centered life. You are on your path and have friends who share the journey. These are friends who have their own paths, but they share the importance of being heart-centered. They cannot walk your path, and you cannot walk theirs, but you share the highway. These friends are good, supportive company. They may stumble along the way, just as you might. You can help pick each other up, but you each have to walk your own path. Now, this highway, Adam, has many diversions."

"Do you mean side roads, or dead ends that lead you away from the highway? And U-turns that lead you in the opposite direction?"

"Exactly. And you could even end up at the county dump," he laughed." But seriously, a dominant mind will lead you into all kinds of dead end traps. Then you become convinced that the dead end you are following is really leading you somewhere important. People often spend their entire lives doing this, and fail to realize what they are looking for all along, is simply their own heart. Adam, let's be realistic. You are going to get sidetracked from time to time. There are lessons to learn on these off-track adventures. That is okay because it is all a part of the journey. There are always lessons in what we call mistakes."

"And the key," I said, "is to learn those lessons, return to your heart, and get back on the highway."

"Yes. You got it! At times you will forget this, but you will wake up, get your bearings, and get back on the highway. The innate wisdom of your heart is guiding and supporting you, but you have to be willing to listen to your heart, or else your choices will take you down dead end roads."

"It feels sooooo good to have a sense of purpose and know that the core of my heart is beautifully connected," I said.

"I know just what you mean, Adam, and I really enjoy being on the highway with you. You are a dear brother to my heart, and I am very happy to be sharing the journey with you."

Chapter Thirty-Six
SCARED OF THE BRICK WALL

When I awoke the next morning, Grandfather was busy hauling boxes out of a back room of the cabin. He said he was moving them out to the new storage shed we had built. I offered to help.

"Great!" he said, heading out the door with an armload of old shoeboxes. I picked up a big cardboard box and the bottom of the box gave out, dropping the entire contents to the floor. I taped the box back together and while I was repacking it, I came across an old black-and-white snapshot of Grandfather Sage as a young man. He was propped up in a hospital bed and surrounded by a bunch of other young guys in military uniforms.

"I didn't know you'd been in a war, Gramps," I said, when he came back in. "What happened to you?"

"I was wounded pretty badly, Adam. I was in that hospital for three months. That picture was taken just before I was released and sent home." He sat down while I finished packing the box.

"You know, Adam, at times life itself seems like a battle. And, along the way, we get wounded."

"I know what you mean. I feel like my wounds haven't healed."

"We each have our own unique set of wounds. We all have our own stories. When we do not heal our wounds, we carry them around with us and they affect how we see things, and how we feel and react to life. Wounds come from many sources," he continued. "They may develop if we do not feel the nurturing and support we would like to have as we grow. If we feel betrayed or violated we develop wounds. We have wounds of un-forgiveness toward ourselves, and toward others. Our resume of wounds goes way, way back and the people who have been cruel to us are often mean because they themselves are very wounded."

"Are you saying their meanness is a reaction from their hurt and wounded self?"

"Yes, that's it. And if they had been living a heart-centered life, they would have responded differently."

"Grandfather, I feel my oldest wounds are wounds of rejection. They're also wounds of feeling I'm not good enough, as if there's something I should be doing better, and I don't even know what that something is."

"I am glad to hear you say that because it is a big step to be open to examining our wounds. Adam, are you aware that it takes a certain amount of energy to hold onto those wounds? You have to hold a lid down on them, you know. They also block the gentleness of Love from being able to give you the best of the best."

"What do you mean, 'hold a lid down'?'"

"Feel deep inside, and you will feel it for yourself."

As I turned my attention inward, I could sense that I had a storage space with a lid on it holding down unresolved parts of myself. It felt like pressure or raw heaviness deep inside the back and bottom of my non-physical heart. "This is where my wounds are stored," I thought.

"You're right," I said. "I'm holding down a lot of stuff. But you gotta be a little nuts, Gramps, if you think I'm going down in the basement to look at that stuff."

"You know, if our basement foundation is shaky it affects the solidity of the building."

"But Gramps, I don't think you understand! If I ever took that lid off I might go over the edge."

"Why is that?"

"My father and all of his put-downs are there. The only emotion I ever felt from him was anger. Whenever anything went wrong he made me think it was my fault, and now I feel it was my fault that he died. Bill's down there, too. He died because I gave him my seat in the front of the car. There's a part of me that feels so raw I just want to cover it up. You're crazy if you think I'm going to take that lid off," I said vehemently. "There's no telling what might happen. If I let down that wall, I will feel the hurt again, and it'll probably feel even worse than it did before."

"Adam, you have a brick wall built up around parts of yourself, and you've convinced yourself it is there for your protection. From your response, it is obvious that your mind thinks it would be a terrible and scary thing if that brick wall was dissolved."

"Duh," I said in frustration.

"So, Adam, was that 'duh' from your head or your heart."

"I've already taken down some of those bricks, but there's no way I'm going to remove the whole wall. I'd feel unprotected."

"I understand, Adam. How about we do an experiment? I promise we won't take the wall down."

Grandfather guided me to let the True Source of Unconditional Love remove my fear so that I could feel the true heart feelings. He then asked me to feel the wall, and all of the hurt and anger stored inside. I could feel my heart contract and a place that felt so heavy, lonely and disconnected. Then he asked my heart to feel what it would be like if these stuck places were dissolved. It was amazing to feel how my heart kept opening more and more, and the peace, joy and gentleness of Love was able to radiate freely.

"Adam, it is important to feel protected. Do you feel that brick wall is the best type of protection? The brick wall is quite cumbersome to carry around, and sitting on that lid takes a lot of energy. To be honest, it is really just a garbage can and everything inside has been rotting. It is a lonely and isolated type of protection. It blocks your deeper heart connection. The best protection and the greatest joy is to live a heart-centered life guided by the innate wisdom of your heart. But these blockages you sense are interfering with your ability to do that properly."

"Well, what do we do with the wounds?" I asked cautiously.

"When you have physical wounds you cleanse them. Likewise, you're mental and emotional wounds need to be cleansed. Wounds are constricted energy patterns that keep you from waking up and being who you really are. They hide and form our shadow. They show up in our hurts and our defenses, and in the ways our buttons get pushed. They color our vision. Emotions arise without your permission. They may range from getting angry with little cause, to feeling easily hurt, aloof or inadequate. When you attempt to get a closer look at the wounds, they typically retreat back into the shadows. Fear can be their food. Also, when you get defensive or hurt, that can feed your wounds, and they seem to thrive even more."

I couldn't imagine how I could possibly cleanse these wounds. As I felt fear come up in me, I started thinking that Gramps was a con and I better protect myself or I'd get tricked into something really stupid that I would regret. He noticed the troubled look on my face and smiled. I could feel his non-judgment, and realized he was radiating such beautiful sweet love. How could this be bad, I wondered? I relaxed, smiled to my heart and began to feel the deep peace and calm. I was able to feel how my head was feeding me this nonsense about Grandfather. The garbage can wanted to remain as a garbage can. It was like an old pattern inviting me to fall back into the hole.

"Adam, I have some really good news for you."

"What's that," I asked.

"It is not your responsibility to get rid of your garbage."

"I'm not responsible to cleanse my wounds?"

"Your only responsibility is to feel the true heart feelings and be grateful to your connection with the True Source of Love. When you are grateful for the Gift, you say 'I do' to being unconditionally loved, and it will keep growing and radiating. It is this Gift that will cleanse and dissolve the stuck energy patterns. The Source of Love wants your heart happy and free so that you can enjoy being a conduit and your presence becomes a healing balm for others."

"Are you sure about that?" I asked

Grandfather laughed. "I am absolutely sure. The True Source of Unconditional Love wants to remove all of our stuck places, so that we can be an instrument of the gentleness of Love, just as we were designed to be. If we hold on to our wounds we will live as our dominant mind and will never know our true self."

"Why would the Source of Love be so interested in my wounds?" I asked.

"Oh Adam, this Gift beyond all Gifts never wants you to live in separation...... only to be within the Unconditional embrace of Love so you can fulfill your deepest purpose on earth. This precious Gift is waiting to dissolve the wounds from your past and the negative emotions you create in your daily life. But you have to be a willing participant. It is your wounds and thinking that you are your dominant mind that keeps you blocked and separate from being unconditionally loved."

"A part of me feels unworthy of being loved completely, and I still feel blocked with the idea that we can really be loved unconditionally."

"Our mind cannot conceive how there can be Unconditional Love for every being, no matter what they have ever done. Only the gratitude in our heart can begin to grasp the depths of what this means. When we are willing to let go and let the True Source of Love help us, patterns are softened and dissolved along with our history of scars. All wounds can be healed, and you can actually really enjoy the process."

"Enjoy healing my wounds and all the pain and scars? Give me a break Gramps!"

"Please let your head withhold judgment, Adam. I can understand this idea is a stretch for you. It was for me. But you will know for yourself in due time. Remember – the fun has just begun. Now let's get the rest of these boxes out of here so you can move into your new room."

"My new room?" I asked in surprise. I'd been sleeping on a cot in the hallway since I'd arrived. I walked over to the window and looked out at a fantastic view of the mountain ridges to the north. Tears began to well up in my eyes. "Thank you very much, Grandfather." He gave me a hug, and we hauled out the last few boxes.

As I moved my things into my new room, I felt a new start in my life had truly begun. The room, even though it was small, looked bare with only my cot and a small chest in it. The room was like me, it seemed – practically empty and waiting to be filled with good things. Now I'm beginning to think like Grandfather, I thought, laughing to myself.

Chapter Thirty-Seven
SHOCK

One morning I wandered down to the river and strolled upstream toward the waterfall, and there was Grandfather doing his dance with nature. He would move his arms and legs about in a slow rhythm, as if he were telling a story with his body. One of the things that most fascinated me about him was how healthy he was. He was very agile. He moved his body gracefully, and had endless energy. I was feeling in a stuck place but didn't want him to know.

"That's some dance you're doing there, Grandfather."

"I am just enjoying the beautiful day, and feeling so grateful for so many wonderful things. By the expression on your face, I can tell that you are not feeling very grateful."

"Huh?"

"You cannot be grateful when you are in your head. You can only be truly grateful when you are enjoying your heart. That's why it is called heart felt gratitude."

"There is no way I can be grateful all the time," I blurted.

"Well Adam, how about for now you consider most of the time. That look on your face says you are on a merry go round, going through your play book of excuses."

"This is the deal, Gramps. I just can't get over this idea that I'm not my brain. I use my brain all the time and think thoughts with my head. I would fail all my classes if I just felt my heart. My brain is real, and it's me."

"If you say so, Adam. By the way, I am going to town soon, and I would like you to join me and help with some errands. Can you do me a favor and get a dozen apples from the tree and also pick a bunch of strawberries from the patch? Put them in a bag because we will take them to town with us."

After breakfast we got in his truck and headed to town. Grandfather asked me to drop off the bag of apples and strawberries to his old friend, John Rivers, who was a resident in the Mountain Ridge Nursing Home. He asked me to introduce myself to John and spend some time visiting since he did not get many visitors. I walked into John's room and told him I was living with Grandfather Sage over at LotusHeart Cabin. John greeted me with a huge smile and said, "A friend of

Sage is a friend of mine."

For the next hour John shared with me stories about when he and Grandfather were in the army together, places they traveled and things they did. John shared with me the history of his amazing life including hard times and great times. I felt I could have listened to John's stories much longer but it was time for me to leave. I was supposed to meet Grandfather over at the post office at 11:30AM.

"Did you enjoy meeting and hanging out with my buddy, John?"

"What a great down to earth guy," I exclaimed. "I learned so much about cultures from other countries, life before I was born, and also some interesting things about you."

"So glad to hear that, Adam. I had a feeling you guys would have a good connection. Can you do me one more favor? I still have some errands to run. When I was at the supermarket I bought some ripe mangoes. Can you run back over to Mountain Ridge and drop off a couple of mangoes to John and tell him that they are a gift from you?"

"Sure, Grandfather." I grabbed two mangoes and looked forward to seeing John again. I knocked on his door, and he asked me to enter.

"Hi John, I brought you a couple of really nice mangoes for you to enjoy."

"Ah, thanks for the mangoes, but who are you?"

"I'm Adam."

"Am I supposed to know you from somewhere?" he asked.

"Quit playing with my head John."

"No, you quit playing with my head and acting like you know me. I don't know any Adam, and now I am wondering if you are trying to rip me off. Please get out of my room."

I was shocked and kept trying to convince myself that he was joking, but he had a very stern look on his face. I tried to say something but he began to stutter and tremble.

Then with a distressed voice he blurted out,

"Young man, get out of here immediately before I throw you out!"

I dropped the mangoes on his bed and ran out the door.

Chapter Thirty-Eight
BRAIN

I got into the truck and said to grandfather, "You are never going to believe what happened to me. I feel so confused and can't make any sense of what happened."

"Adam, sometimes confusion can be good. I have a feeling that your confusion is serving you well."

"Quit this mumbo jumbo stuff, Gramps. This is serious."

"You know brother, your biggest problem is that sometimes you are not confused enough."

"What are you talking about? I told you this is serious. Why are you laughing?"

"I am laughing because sometimes I can help you so much more when you are confused. When you are not confused and stuck in your head, you often feel so justified in what you think and believe. There is little room for change because your heart is closed and your mind is dominant. Your confusion has just cracked a hole in your head and you are not as head strong as you were this morning."

"Okay, I hear you, but I got to tell you what happened."

"Do me a favor, Adam. Just sit on it for awhile. Get out of your head and into your heart. Reflect over what happened. I will make us a nice lunch and that will give you some time for things to soften. I am curious to see what realizations you come up with."

I sat under the willow tree and leaned against the trunk. I started to question, "How could John have been so friendly toward me and then become so angry and not know who I was?" I touched my heart, relaxed and could feel the true heart feelings becoming gentler and sublime. My heart asked for understanding. I began to realize that who I connected with as 'John' was so much more than just his brain. I felt a deep heart to heart connection that was real and felt grateful for what he shared with me. I let the True Source of Unconditional Love remove my confusion and anxiety. As I could feel the burden and distress lift, I began to feel insights flowing from the innate wisdom of my heart. I realized that John was a wonderful man, and that something with his brain was not working correctly. Wow! Suddenly I understood that he had a brain but he was so much more than a brain. The real John is the core of his heart. I began to chuckle remembering how I began this morning arguing with Grandfather and telling him that 'my brain is real and my brain is me'. Grandfather had a

107

great salad sprinkled with walnuts and almonds waiting for us when I got to the kitchen. We ate without talking, and I took Grandfather's cue to be grateful while enjoying each bite of our salad. After eating we went out to the porch to sit in the rocking chairs.

"Adam, what would you like to share with me?"

I explained what happened when I went back to give John the mangoes, and how he did not know me. I shared how painful it felt when he threw me out of his room.

"What have you concluded?" he asked.

"I now realize we are more than our brains. My heart was able to feel how my brain is not the real me just as John's brain is not the real John. Our brain is a tool to help us express ourselves on earth, but we can only know our real selves through the door of our hearts. I remembered when you once told me that the destiny of all brains is the graveyard, but the heart is the door to our true self. I feel that I understand that now."

"Good conclusion young man!"

"I still can't understand why John did not recognize me when I came back with the mangoes."

"Adam, you are right. The brain is a tool to serve us so we can function. We have short term and long term memory. John's long term memory is working perfectly fine. He has excellent recall of the past."

"Yes, he does. I was amazed at the details he shared about the times the two of you had together 40 years ago. He feels such a loving, brotherly connection with you, Grandfather."

"I feel the same for John. With age everyone's brain goes through a certain amount of deterioration. John's short term memory has severely deteriorated as he has aged. The first time you met John, he got to meet you because he knows me from the past. When you went back to give John the mangoes, he was meeting you for the first time because his short term memory is not able to remember you."

"It is so clear that we are more than our brain", I exclaimed.

"I'm so happy to hear you say that, Adam."

108

Chapter Thirty-Nine
RESOLUTION

We were walking along the river one afternoon after finishing a project, when we heard a screeching sound above us. We looked up but could see only a patch of blue sky through the treetops. Grandfather said it was the unmistakable call of the bald eagle, something he'd rarely heard in that part of the woods.

"The sounds of nature are voices from the Gift of Unconditional Love, Adam. They offer us wonderful gifts."

"What kinds of gifts?"

"You will learn to recognize them over time. The sounds of the songbirds offer our ears a gift. The sound of the ocean waves soothes us and the sounds of gushing rivers and waterfalls remind our hearts to be grateful for all of the natural wonders. Without a grateful heart, we can never be happy."

We sat down at a place where the river narrowed to about half its width. A small set of rapids rushed over the rocks.

"It is easy to let go of our old stuck patterns here," Grandfather said. We sat for a long time watching the water bubble over the rocks. I became absorbed in the cleansing sound of the river.

We heard the cry of the eagle again, and this time, when we looked up we saw two of them. Grandfather pointed out a young eagle following its parent. They circled directly above us, and then flew away, following the river upstream. I watched them in awe.

"Come with me, Adam."

"Where are we going, Grandfather?"

"I am taking you to my favorite healing place."

We climbed the rocks to the top of the waterfall and followed the river upstream. Oak and willow trees branched out over the water from both sides of the river, creating a shady canopy. As I looked ahead, a huge boulder caught my eye. I felt magnetically drawn to it.

"You are feeling the connection, Adam. It is no coincidence you feel drawn to that boulder. That is where we are going."

As we approached the boulder I could feel its presence. "This may sound crazy," I said, "but I get the feeling this boulder knows we're here."

Grandfather laughed.

"How do you know it doesn't, Adam?" We climbed up and sat on the top of the boulder. "I come here from time to time. Resolution is my good friend."

"Who is Resolution?" I asked.

"You felt Resolution's presence when you approached her. Now you are sitting on her lap."

"Do you mean you think this rock is alive?" I asked.

"It is somewhat difficult to explain my relationship with Resolution. To me, she has a presence that is very real. My sense is that Resolution has an ancient history, and for thousands of years many Native Americans came to sit here during healing ceremonies. Over the years I have come here during times when I was confused or seeking solutions to difficult situations. And I have come here many times when I felt called to do a personal retreat and express deep gratitude for the Gift of Unconditional Love."

"What do you do when you come here?"

"I sit on her lap, like we are now, and let my innate heart wisdom guide what happens next. She offers me inspiration. She has been quite a gracious host for all these years."

"I can feel that, Grandfather. She sure is a wonderful expression of nature. How did she get the name 'Resolution?' "

"One day I sat enjoying the awe of nature, and all of a sudden my heart felt that her name is Resolution. That is what I have been calling her ever since."

"Does Grandmother Gabriella know about Resolution?"

"Yes, she does, Adam. She does not come here, though. She has her own boulder friend she visits."

"It sounds like you've never brought anyone here before. I feel like I'm invading a private relationship."

"That's sensitive of you, Adam, and I appreciate your courtesy. But I have brought you here for a reason. You are here so I can introduce you to Resolution. The two of you have already become acquainted, and I am happy I chose to share this special place with you."

"But this is your place."

"Well, Adam, my time on this planetary school-house is limited. I will be leaving earth school long before you. But Resolution will still be here. If you find yourself struggling with an issue, or just feeling stuck, you can come and sit in Resolution's lap. It is a wonderful place to let the gentleness of Love heal our wounds. Some of my most profound moments have taken place right at this spot."

"I don't know what to say, Grandfather. Thank you for offering to share this special place with me. I feel I'll be spending some time here, too."

"In time your relationship with this special spot will grow, Adam, and you will be grateful for having such a nourishing friend."

My heart felt at such peace there. When we got up to leave, I said good-bye to Resolution. As I walked away, I had a feeling I'd made a connection with a special place and a friend I knew I'd visit again.

Chapter Forty
LIVING WITH GRATITUDE

"What are you building now, Gramps?" He was whistling a tune as he cut and sanded some boards.

"New bat houses, Adam. I like to keep as many bats as I can in the area."

"Well, it looks like you're enjoying yourself and doing a great job", I said.

"Have you ever had a job, Adam?"

"Sure. I've stocked shelves in a supermarket, and I've washed dishes in a restaurant."

"What did you like most about working?"

"Getting paid, of course," I chuckled.

"Oh? Why did you like to get paid?"

"Why would I work if it wasn't for the pay?" I exclaimed.

"So, Adam, your pay is your reward, and work is what you have to do to get it."

"That's right."

"Adam, what do you do when you get paid?"

"Well, I go to the movies, or buy a pizza or something like that."

"How long does the movie last?"

"About two hours, Gramps."

"How long does it take to eat your pizza?"

"I can eat half a pizza in five minutes when I'm hungry."

"So Adam, which takes more time? The work or the reward?"

"What do you mean?"

"Your two-hour movie and ten-minute pizza take a lot less time than working all week to get a paycheck. Soon your overhead will be much larger than it is now."

"Well, I never really thought of it like that, but I do see your point."

"Most of us have been conditioned from a young age to seek rewards. We have to figure out how to stop separating work from rewards," Grandfather explained.

"But what's wrong with rewards, Gramps?"

"There is nothing wrong with rewards. The problem is in living our lives only to enjoy rewards. When our mind is overly dominant, we get good at doing this. We have been conditioned to perform tasks not for the enjoyment or appreciation of the process, but for the reward that follows."

"So the problem with having the reward as our focus is that we miss the enjoyment of the process itself?," I asked.

"That's right. One of the keys to a fulfilling life is overcoming the distinction between what you consider a chore and what you consider a reward. The best reward that you can reap is when you are heartfully engaged with gratitude in whatever you are doing. You are in the here and now, enjoying your heart in all that you do. Being grateful in each moment and even for all small things is so very wonderful."

"I've experienced some of that Grandfather. When gathering rocks to rebuild your wall, I was really enjoying gathering the rocks and carrying them. It felt fun."

"Life becomes much more entertaining when we stop separating work from rewards, Adam. Rewards provide only temporary pleasure. If you have not figured that out, much of your life will seem like a burden. Do you know what happens if you indulge in a pleasure long enough?"

"It will lose its attraction", I said.

"Yes, and it can even become boring after a while. But as we learn to be heart centered all that we do can be enjoyable, even those things that your head may not like to do. We lose the distinction between work, chores and rewards. We live not only to seek pleasure..."

"We live to live", I blurted out.

"Right, Adam! We live a heart-centered life with gratitude and our connection with the True Source of Unconditional Love brings such wonderful joy, and the deepest fulfillment."

Chapter Forty-One
PERMANENT RESIDENT OF LOVE

We were shoveling compost into a new garden bed on an unusually warm day, and I stopped to rest for a moment. Grandfather saw me panting and jokingly called me a wimp. I could see the smirk on his face and knew he was teasing me again.

When we got back to the cabin, I challenged him to an arm wrestle. I was good at arm wrestling, and wanted to see how he would handle losing. I thought at his age, there was no way he could beat me.

We sat down at the table and our right hands embraced. I couldn't believe it. His arm locked like a bar of steel. I was unable to budge it. He calmly ate an apple with his other hand, chewing each bite slowly. I was sure he could have put my arm down with ease, but he chose to hold a locked position. After a few minutes, I told him I'd had enough. He didn't have to call me a wimp. I felt like one.

"Do you know what the problem is with focusing on what you are afraid might happen?" he asked. "You put energy into what you fear. That increases the probability of it coming true."

"Like if I'm afraid I'm going to run into a snake, it might happen?"

"Yes. You might even create a snake out of a hose. Thinking is an action, and our actions have impact. When you think, your thoughts become a part of life. The question is what kind of impact are you creating?"

Grandfather became very serious and stared into my eyes. I knew he had something important to say.

"Adam, the quality of your thoughts when your head is in charge, is very different from the quality of your thoughts when you are heart centered. A lot of our problems and burdens are created and sustained by the kinds of thoughts we think and emotions we experience when we are mind dominant.

"Your thoughts have the capacity to attract and manifest circumstances. Be careful what you think. When you are in your heart, your thoughts will be congruent. When you're grounded in your heart, you do not produce negative thoughts and emotions. You only do that when your head is in charge. That's why I said, you cannot contaminate the energy field of your heart when you are in your heart. You only dirty your heart when your head is the boss and the ego is in charge. Even if you are having negative emotions while keeping your mouth shut and not expressing them out loud, you still create clouds that block the radiance of your true heart feelings."

"What a drag, Gramps. I was hoping that if I did not emotionally dump on someone, then it did not count."

"Silence does not save you. If you think it, you will have negative emotions and your heart experiences the consequence which is more clouds in the sky and feeling less radiance from the sun."

"Its wonderful news that we don't dirty our heart or create negative emotions when we are grounded in our hearts", I said.

"That's right, Adam. You become an instrument in motion. The heart is grateful as you enjoy peace, calm and joy. And that has a positive effect on your relationships and environment."

"What if someone does something you don't like, and you say, 'What a jerk. I hope he breaks his leg?' "

"Then immediately recognize that you have engaged in a negative thought. That lets you know that you are in a mind dominant space. Relax, smile and return to your heart by enjoying the nice feelings from your heart. Remember your great teacher is in front of you."

"What do you mean 'great teacher'. The guy is an idiot."

"He who makes you the angriest is your greatest teacher."

We both laughed.

"Adam, it is important to recognize when you are in negative thoughts and disconnected from your heart connection. The quality of thoughts you are directing toward others may not be of a proper quality. When people exchange negative thoughts with each other, they are engaging in a form of psychic warfare. They may not realize it, but they are playing in the dark, and the consequences can be damaging."

"I prefer not to play that game anymore. And it's not fun."

"I know that, Adam, and it makes me feel very good when I realize how much you have progressed. We are learning to live heart-centered lives. Our challenge is to not just be in temporary connection with the True Source of Unconditional

Love, but to live with our whole heart, whole being and physical form within the connection ....and to let this be our Home rather than a place we visit."

Wow... to be a permanent resident of our heart. Tears began to silently stream down from my eyes. I felt deeply touched, and I was so grateful that I understood more about the path of the heart and all that was to come.

Chapter Forty-Two
BLOCKAGES SURFACING

Over the next few days I spent a lot of time alone practicing what Grandfather had taught me about the heart. I was feeling more and more grateful for even small things that I previously would never notice. It was getting easier to tell when I was in my heart and when my mind was dominant. In fact it was obvious, and what I used to think was my normal mental state, began to feel strange and awkward. Being in my heart and enjoying the wonderful feelings began to feel more and more natural. I no longer thought the real me was my head. I realized that my essence, or who I really am, is connected to the core of my heart. Deep inside, I felt pressure and blockages so I continued letting the True Source of Unconditional Love remove stuck emotions while also forgiving others and my-self. I began to realize what an amazing gift it is to have our garbage replaced by love and gratefulness. I became aware of deeper layers in my heart that needed to be cleansed, and I knew these were the clouds that Grandfather was talking about that limit the quality of how the joyful gentleness of Love is able to radiate. I understood that at some point these blockages would need to be cleansed, but I didn't want to face them.

"Grandfather, I am so much enjoying my heart but I can feel these blockages surfacing and I'm not in the mood to deal with them."

"That's okay. Knowing there are blockages waiting to be cleansed is a good sign. It means that you are relaxed and enjoying the true heart feelings. Love is gently pushing against the edges of your blockages. As I shared before, the Source of Love always wants our whole heart, whole being and even our physical form to be within the direct Love connection. Right now, you can feel the gentleness of Love inside of you, but all of you is not yet within that Love."

"I am not sure I am ready for all parts of me to be like that."

"Adam, the True Source of Love always wants to give us the best. That can only happen when we continue to enjoy our heart connection. Adam, when you are ready, it will happen."

"I'm glad to hear that Grandfather. I am not in the mood to be pushed."

"The good news, Adam, is that the Gift of Unconditional Love will never push you because Love is always the most gentle. You must be a willing participant to enjoy more and more. The depth of your heart experience is limited by how much you are willing to accept. The more you are willing, without any effort, to enjoy the gentleness of Love, the more it can help you."

"I still have a part of me that feels unworthy of feeling and enjoying more and more Love," I said. "I don't know why but that feeling of inadequacy is just there. It's as if enjoying more than I already do would make me feel guilty."

"Your guilt and shame are simply blockages in your heart that will need to be cleansed", Grandfather reassured me. "The Source of Love is all Loving, even in our darkest moments."

"I hear you, but I have trouble accepting it."

"Adam, if a loving mother has two children and one child stays clean and the other child always gets dirty in the mud, doesn't the mother still love the child who gets dirty? And doesn't the mother want to pick up the child from the mud and clean him, cuddle him, and tuck him into a warm bed?"

I began to quietly sob because my heart knew this story was a metaphor of how we are loved completely. I heard it and began to believe it, but I could not yet fully feel it.

"Adam, let's go for a walk, and hang up some of our new bat houses while we talk, shall we?" We walked into the woods down the hill from the cabin where it was cool and shady.

This was an area I hadn't explored much. I wandered around while Grandfather did all the work of putting up the bat houses. I found a small stream that must have fed into the river. I sat down there on a soft bed of fallen pine needles. Grandfather joined me a few minutes later.

"Adam, you are ready to begin fulfilling your deeper purpose in life."

"Wonderful, what is it?" .

"Adam, in all my years I have never found a U-haul truck brings someone's possessions to the graveyard when they die. You are born in your birthday suit, and you leave earth empty handed of all things. No matter how much you gather, you do not get to take it with you. But you do take the quality of your heart."

Grandfather continued. "You've heard me say this before. You are here on earth, as we all are, to become an instrument as the True Source of Love intends for us to be."

"Yes, Grandfather, I've heard you say that many times, but how do I do that?"

"By accepting, enjoying and being grateful for Unconditional Love, so that the gentleness of Love can radiate in all directions to be shared with everyone," he exclaimed.

118

Then Grandfather had me close my eyes, relax, enjoy and feel the love radiating from my heart. He guided me to smile to every heart everywhere. I could feel the sweetness from the gentleness of Love radiating and expanding. It felt as if the edges and boundaries that kept me feeling I had to protect my personal space were dissolving, and that felt so freeing. It was wonderful to feel that my heart was a conduit so that the gentleness of Love could radiate. My heart longed for more and to never feel separate or far away from the Gift of Unconditional Love ever again.

Chapter Forty-Three
AN INSTRUMENT FOR THE
TRUE SOURCE OF LOVE

I was beginning to see myself, and life, in a new way. Just being in nature, without television, radio, or even newspapers, made me realize how caught up I had always been with one distraction or another. I now developed appreciation and gratitude for simple and natural things in life, such as humming birds, cloud formations, swaying trees in the wind, hooting owls, and flower fragrances in the air.

One day late in the afternoon, I was heading back to the cabin feeling exhilarated but exhausted, after a full day of hiking. I stumbled over a stick in my path. I thought this was a sign that it might be a good idea to stop and rest for a few minutes. I plopped down and picked up the stick. It was about four feet long. I removed some loose bark and took out my pocketknife and carved some leaf patterns into the wood and decided to give it to Grandfather.

I returned to the cabin to find Grandfather in the midst of laying out a fantastic dinner. He had spent the afternoon baking bread.

"I thought you might be hungry, Adam," he smiled.

I thanked him heartily. After dinner I gave him the walking stick.

"I should be able to get around for many years to come with this," he chuckled. "Thank you, Adam."

"And thank you, Grandfather," He became quiet as he examined my carving on the stick.

"When I was younger, Adam," he said after a few minutes, "I was comfortable with giving, but my problem was I did not feel comfortable receiving. I had to learn to be open to receiving. Learning to do this helped me to find a deeper level of harmony within myself. In every moment Love is Love, and it is important that we learn to accept it."

"How do we do that?" I asked.

"You know the answer to that one."

"By enjoying and being grateful for the Gift of Unconditional Love, I bet," I said.

"Exactly! The more you gratefully enjoy, the more you accept. And the more you enjoy and accept, the more you can share. The gentleness of Love will just radiate without you having to do anything at all except to accept what is freely being given to you in every moment."

"Cool, Grandfather. What a great arrangement that has provided us."

"Yes, it sure beats the model that some humans have created saying you have to suffer or do penance to prove you are worthy of God's Love."

"Why would the Gift of Unconditional Love ever want us to suffer?" I asked.

"The True Source of Love does not want us to suffer and actually wants us to accept, enjoy, and share the gentleness of Love. The problem is that because of our blockages, we are limited in how much we are willing to accept. Are you ready for an experiment?"

"Bring it on, Grandfather."

"I would like you to recall someone who does not push your buttons and who you feel a pretty good connection with."

I remembered a math teacher from last semester. Mr. Kelly was a really nice guy, and I felt he respected me.

"Now pick someone you have issues with."

"That's easy. I have a list to choose from." I remembered Vinnie who was a few years older, and how he picked on me whenever he had the chance.

"Relax, smile, and let your heart realize that love is radiating. Now let your heart smile to Mr. Kelly. Feel what is happening. How is your heart responding? How is the love radiating? Now let your heart smile to Vinnie. How is your heart responding and how is the gentleness of Love radiating?"

"What a difference! That was amazing. When my heart smiled to Mr. Kelly, I could feel how the gentleness radiated smoothly and freely. When my heart smiled to Vinnie, the vibration felt much denser. It just didn't radiate freely the way it did with Mr. Kelly."

"What a great realization, Adam. Can you explain why?"

"Probably because I did not have any significant problems with Mr. Kelly, so there were no unresolved issues to block or filter the radiance. Now with Vinnie, I still have unresolved emotions so as I tried to smile to his heart, the radiance had to pass through my blockages. I suppose that slowed down the vibration."

"What a wonderful explanation, Adam. We are ready for part two of the experiment. Let the Unconditional Love from the True Source of Love help you to forgive Vinnie for everything he did to hurt you or harm you in any way. Now let gentleness of Love remove any remaining disappointments, sadness or resentments regarding your relationship with Vinnie and replace them with love and gratefulness."

As I followed Grandfather's directions, I could feel the old wounds and resentments dissolving that I held for so many years.

"Now let your heart smile to Vinnie. How does that feel? Now let your heart smile to Mr. Kelly. Tell me, what the difference is now."

"There is a huge difference. When I let my heart smile to Vinnie, the gentleness radiates more smoothly and gently. It is not as coarse or slowed down as it was before. But it is still not as free to radiate compared to Mr. Kelly."

"That's because you dissolved some of your issues and related blockages with Vinnie, but not all of them. If you did, the gentleness of Love would radiate with even less limitation.

"So Adam, wouldn't it be fun to make a list of everybody you have ever known, so you can smile to each of their hearts and discover whether you have any unresolved issues with them? Remember, your heart wants to be free to smile sweetly and let the gentleness of Love radiate in all directions, to the heart of every being in all of existence. It is then that you are truly an instrument."

"Grandfather, it is so awesome that by enjoying Love we receive more and more Love, and by accepting we are giving."

"The greatest thing you can give, Adam, is your shining heart which radiates to everyone you are in contact with. Then you are helping to lighten the load of the densities created from a mind dominant world. Your peaceful presence helps to clear the air of its denseness. You provide a cleansing effect to the darker thoughts which also pervade space. When one is grounded in their heart, their connection to the True Source of Love helps to heal disharmonious energies in the environment. What a great gift to share with your friends, family, communities, earth and all of existence!"

Grandfather continued. "We are not here on earth to gather, conquer or achieve more and more. We are here to be instruments for the True Source of Love in sacred partnership. It is our birthright, and it is our ultimate purpose. Let us be grateful for even the smallest of things."

Chapter Forty-Four
BEYOND PERCEPTION

The long, hot summer days made it necessary to water the garden a great deal more than usual. I was watering one evening when Grandfather came out. He strolled slowly up and down the rows with his hands clasped behind him, stopping occasionally to examine a particular plant.

"Adam," he called out from the far corner of the garden, "these watermelon vines would like some more water!"

"I already watered them, Grandfather!" I called back.

"I can see that, but they would really appreciate a little more water!"

"Okay! No problem! Tell them I'll be right over!" I dragged the hose back down the row to where Grandfather was kneeling next to the watermelons.

"If we pick this larger one, Adam, the smaller ones will be happier, and do better."

"I can see their smiling faces already," I joked.

"Oh, yes," he said, thumping the larger one with his knuckle. "Do you hear that, Adam? This one is ripe and ready for consumption. We can have some when you are finished with the watering." He headed back toward the cabin, smiling, and cradling the watermelon in his arms as if it were a newborn baby.

When I had finished the watering, I found Grandfather on the front porch in his rocking chair admiring the watermelon he had placed on the table next to him.

"It sure is a beauty, isn't it, Adam?"

"The prettiest I've seen. So, tell me, Grandfather, how did you know the watermelon plants were so thirsty tonight? You could see the soil was soaked."

"There are ways to see without using our eyes, Adam. Our eyes, ears, nose and tongue are sensory organs we use to take in data from the world. We hear things, smell things, taste things and see things. Right?"

"Yes."

"Our perceptions can be limited to what we are physically capable of perceiving. And if our sensory organs are limited, that means our perception of the world is limited."

"Well, I know our sense of hearing is limited," I said. "My cousin had a dog whistle. When I blew it, his dog could hear it, but we couldn't."

"Right, Adam. Our ears hear only certain frequencies within a particular bandwidth of frequencies. Similarly, our eyes see light waves only within a certain frequency range. When something is out of the range of your eyes' capacity to see it, you might think it doesn't exist."

"So when people say, 'I'll believe it when I see it,' they may not realize they're limiting themselves to what they can see," I shared.

"Yes, and there is more going on in this universe than meets the eye. The deepest realizations can only be known with your inner heart. Our innate heart wisdom allows us to understand and realize hidden and deeper aspects of reality we cannot see with our eyes, or perceive with our other senses. Everything has a different vibration. Every thought, word or feeling has its own vibration."

"I call them good vibes and bad vibes," I said.

"And our heart can sense these vibes, Adam. Our innate heart wisdom allows us to make wise choices and decisions. Our heart allows us to have an inner knowing that is beyond the perception of our senses or comprehension of our brain."

"Yah, Gramps, I know what you mean. There was a guy who tried to become friends with me. I didn't know anything about him, but something in me didn't like his vibes."

"Your heart helped you realize you needed to be cautious of him, Adam. That's why people say 'I knew it deep in my heart or in the core of my heart'. They don't say I knew it in the core of my head." Grandfather sliced open the watermelon and handed me a piece, staring at me as I took a bite. "What does it taste like, Adam?"

"It tastes really good."

"But can you describe the taste so I will know what you are tasting?"

"It's sweet, ya know, and juicy. Like a melon, ya know?"

Grandfather sighed and shook his head. "I don't know what you mean. I guess I will have to taste it myself," he said, slicing off a huge piece. I laughed at him, wondering what he was trying to show me this time.

"Language, as well as our senses, can be limiting, Adam."

"I guess language can take you only so far, Adam replied."

"Awakening to the fullness of the moment and the joy of our inner being is an experience beyond language, beyond words. There is unity within the diversity of life. Language is the means by which we communicate with one another, but it is limited in helping us to experience the deeper reality, the essence of our true self."

"So, Grandfather, the information we take in through our limited senses we then translate into words, and discuss as if we're seeing the whole picture."

"Yes, Adam. Language is important. Without it we would not have had the wonderful conversations we did. But until we are safe to feel and let Love bring us into the core of our heart, we are looking at a very limited picture."

Chapter Forty-Five
GROUNDED IN THE HEART

One day late in the afternoon, we were surprised by a sudden thunderstorm. I had been splitting firewood while Grandfather stacked it in the woodshed. He was teaching me the words to an old-time mountain tune he remembered from his childhood. "People would often sing," he said, "to keep their energy levels up while they worked long days in the summertime."

We were singing loudly, and laughing at the nonsensical lyrics when the wind picked up suddenly, blowing in lots of massive, dark clouds. We heard a clap of thunder and saw a lightning bolt hit the ground. I dropped the ax. Grandfather dropped an armload of wood, and we both ran as fast as we could for the cabin.

After we had caught our breath and relaxed for a few minutes Grandfather disappeared into the huge storage closet off the kitchen. I sat looking out through the screen door and remembered the night I had spent alone out in the woods during the lightning storm. What an ego I'd had! I shook my head. It was almost unbelievable to me how my perceptions had changed since then. Grandfather walked back into the room carrying a small wooden box.

"I feel like I've begun to wake up from a dream," I said. "The funny thing is, I had no idea I was dreaming. When I look back on the way I used to think and act, I'm not sure who that person was."

"Always keep in heart - not in mind," he said with a sly smile, "that we are in process. The True Source of Unconditional Love is giving us the best of the best. Yes, we may look back and see that the way we were is much different than the way we are now. But, guess what? This process will continue. In the future you will look back again, and feel as if this time was a dream. It is important for us to learn to be grateful for even the smallest of things, and to choose the gentleness of love over our right to be judgmental." He opened the box and pulled out a chessboard.

"Well! It looks like playing chess is going to be part of my life today," I grinned. "I think it's only fair to warn you, though. I'm pretty good at it."

Grandfather just smiled and set up the chess pieces.

He won the first game in less than ten minutes. The second game lasted a few minutes longer, but he won again. The thunderstorm had passed over by the time we were on our third game, but a steady rain was falling. I was contemplating what Grandfather's next move would be.

"Checkmate," he said.

"How did you do that again?! Not one of our games has lasted more than fifteen minutes! This is so frustrating!"

"If frustration is what you would like to create with your time, Adam, feel free to elaborate. Would you like to throw something or break anything?"

"No, I'm not that pissed."

"Well, the clock is ticking, Adam."

"What do you mean by that?"

"Every second you are getting one second closer to your physical death. What do you choose to create with your time? Will you accept and let the gentleness of Love give you the best, and will you allow it to radiate so that your life adds a healing fragrance to existence, or will you create a lot of frustrated energy which pollutes space?"

"Okay. I get the picture."

"Adam, have you ever walked into a room where you could feel that it had been contaminated with negative emotional energy?"

"Yes. The room felt very heavy. I didn't feel like staying there."

"That is because the energy of that space did not resonate with your vibration. A lot of emotional dumping may have taken place there. Certain spaces can be carrying a lot of constrictive, sick energy. Your energy field can pick up unwanted debris just like a white coat gets dirty in polluted smog. This happens when you are not properly grounded in your heart."

"Then what would you do if you had to stay there?" I asked.

"You can change and cleanse the vibration of the space."

"How do you do that?"

"Come with me Adam." Grandfather led me into the basement. It had a hard dirt floor. There were no windows. He did not turn on the lights, and it was pitch black. We stood in total darkness.

"Where is the light, Adam?"

"There is none. I can't even see your face." Grandfather turned on the lights, and I could see that we were standing in a bomb shelter.

"Where is the darkness now?" he asked.

"The light has filled the room and the darkness has disappeared. What a cool example! I get it. If I'm in a place that has dark or negative vibrations, letting the gentleness of Love radiate can clear the negativities from that space. Just like when you turned on the light, the darkness in the room disappeared."

"Yes, Adam, but what happens if you are in a negative environment, but you are not grounded in your heart?"

"I expect that you would be vulnerable to picking up or be negatively influenced by those vibrations."

"This is a paradox, Adam. People think they are vulnerable if they open their heart and that by staying closed-hearted and headstrong, they are assuming a safe position that will protect them. It is actually the opposite. The safest place to be is with an open heart because it is the gentleness of Love that opens our heart. That creates a field around you that protects you from the negative energies which exist in space. When you have a closed heart and a strong head, the gentleness of Love is not radiating so you lack a protective field around you. Negative energies from people or places can enter your field and affect you in ways you are not aware of. The real risk is to live with a closed heart."

"What a cool explanation."

Grandfather continued, "If you are not grounded in your heart, you can pick up that negative energy and carry it around with you, and then you run the risk of dumping your pent-up emotions on other people, or holding it in where it might fester. Those negative, festering energies are examples of how we contaminate the energy field of our heart. They become blockages that obstruct the radiance of Love."

"Thank you so much, Grandfather. I am very grateful that you are in my life and sharing so many experiences with me. What a cool sibling you are."

Chapter Forty-Six
OUR TRUE SELF

After dinner that night, we went outside to do some star gazing. We felt in awe as Grandfather explained that we were peeking into a vast space that contains trillions of stars, planets and galaxies beyond our milky way. And here we sit on earth gyrating through space in a classroom we call life.

I asked, "Why have so many people throughout history been killed in the name of God?"

"Sometimes people think they are following what God wants and think that they are actually following their heart. But they are stuck in their head and self-righteously following their emotions, beliefs and false concepts. If they learned to truly follow their heart, they would not engage in behaviors that harmed others. And do not let your heart forget Adam that they too are our siblings, or else we will get pulled out of our heart by our judgments. As more hearts accept the Gift of Unconditional Love, a planetary shift will continue to unfold. More and more hearts will be able to easily and naturally awaken through the Gift of Unconditional Love."

Grandfather continued, "Different cultures and religions have different names for God and different ways of expressing their worship, but the Gift of Love is for everyone. Adam, there is a unity that exists within diversity. When people forget this, they get caught up in experiencing only the diversity and separation. They may fight with the pieces that look different from their own and fail to experience the sacred interconnection of life. When people's minds are dominant, they are cut off from the innate wisdom of their hearts and that sets the stage for self-righteous thinking and judgmental thoughts."

I pondered that and said, "Maybe it's their wounds and their conditioning that limits their perspective. They feel separation because they experience their world from their heads instead of their hearts."

"Exactly, Adam. We are all part of sacred fabric held together by the True Source of Unconditional Love. Being in our heart allows us to not get caught up in judging people's faults and idiosyncrasies. We can accept their imperfections without getting our buttons pushed."

"Grandfather, now I have begun to realize what this really means."

"It's so wonderful to hear that Adam. As you become more and more grounded in your heart, you can consciously experience the essence of your being. Your true self, the real you, your spirit, resides in the core of your heart. Our journey is about waking up and being who we really are. All the roles we act out in life are simply roles we play, but the roles are not the real us. People fail to realize this and become identified with these roles. Our true self, is beyond all of those roles, yet while we are living in the world, we get to learn lessons from the assortment of roles we play. Whether the role is as a son, brother, student, father, husband, worker, boss, friend, neighbor, leader, or follower, these roles provide wonderful opportunities. Every moment is a chance to choose to gratefully enjoy and accept the Gift of Unconditional Love, so that our hearts can open more. Through this process the real us can emerge. My dear brother, we are not here on earth to enhance our name or fame. We are not here to gain more power or control. We are in earth school to awaken our true being and to live as we truly are."

"Grandfather, what a relief to realize I don't have to become or be anybody special. Got a ways to go, but I am on the highway and getting closer. I can feel how being in our heart allows us to step back and detach from all of our created roles and conditioning."

"That's right, Adam. For example, when my mother was alive I got to play the role of her son. I fulfilled the responsibilities of that role to serve my mother. Though on a deeper level, my heart knew that she is a fellow pilgrim and we are all like siblings."

"That makes a lot of sense," I said. "If we are all siblings, then your mother would also be like your sister."

After a pause, I asked, "Grandfather, how can I become my true self?" He replied, "What I am going to say is hard for many to understand because they think that the deepest spiritual awakening comes from their personal efforts to get better and better. Many people continue to think "if only I can get good enough and be better than I already am, then I can achieve a greater state of spiritual mastery." But Adam, Unconditional Love is not achieved and it is not earned because it has no conditions. We are learning to rely on our hearts connection with the True Source of Unconditional Love so that the gentleness of Love can remove the patterns that keep us separated from who we really are. It is through the process of accepting the Gift of Unconditional Love that we fulfill the spiritual dimension of life so that our true self can be revealed.

"It is a process, Adam, and you are doing wonderfully. Allow your heart to continue opening by enjoying and being grateful. As you keep accepting the Gift of Love, the gentleness of Love removes our blockages and limitations. As your heart keeps opening in all directions, boundaries and limitations dissolve. This is the process of how your true self awakens. At present, your true self is confined because of all of those blockages that are still in your heart and surrounding the core. Old unresolved emotions and issues along with parts of ourselves that do not feel worthy of being loved completely are keeping the real us in a contracted state. Your non-physical heart has multiple layers with many blockages. So be patient with the process. Just keep gratefully enjoying your heart and share the gentleness of Love as an instrument by letting it effortlessly radiate. The rest shall unfold."

I chuckled as I shared with grandfather, "Oh my, if my friends from the neighborhood could hear us talking now, they would really think I am crazy." We both had a good laugh.

Chapter Forty-Seven
LOVE WILL GIVE US THE BEST

I stood barefoot, watching the waterfall early one morning. Everything felt alive and vibrant. After taking a dip in the river I felt completely refreshed and could sense how Native Americans would have loved this spot for fishing and bathing. I sat on the river bank and was happy about how easy it had become to enjoy my heart. All I had to do is relax and smile to my heart, and I could instantly feel the gentleness of Love radiating. I felt a presence to my right. I opened my eyes and was pleased to see Grandfather sitting next to me. I knew he was being an instrument, and could feel the gentleness of Love emanating from his heart. We sat in silence enjoying together for over an hour. Then I began to feel a lot of emotions surfacing and a deep pressure inside my heart. I experienced being extremely stuck inside and felt like a dam was getting ready to burst. It surprised me, and I felt myself shift out of my heart and into my head. I was scared that the dam would release a flood of uncontrollable emotions. What if I got so out of control that I get sucked in a whirlpool and could not get out of that dark, frigid water? I shared my concerns and fears with Grandfather.

"What a magnificent day, Adam," he responded brightly. "I do understand your fears and concerns very well because I went through them myself. Before your head convinces you that it is safer to retreat to the mind-dominant way of thinking, I would like to share something. Everyone is looking for their heart, yet they do not realize it. They continue to look for Love in the wrong places as the old song says. They endeavor to find happiness and joy through people, places or things - all temporary pleasures and they confuse them with authentic happiness. They fail to find the happiness and joy that only our hearts can experience. There is nothing wrong with the material world but when you expect or look toward it for your fulfillment, it will lead you down dead end streets with lots of holes in the road along the way."

"I know the holes and dead end streets you're talking about, but I'm scared."

"Adam, I remember some of those holes in your old path, and I am grateful that you were able to change direction and get back on the highway toward Home. You have come such a long way. Now you are on the verge of another fork in the road."

"I can feel the fork, Grandfather. One part of me wants to go forward on the path of the heart. The other part of me wants to run away. I don't want to face all those blockages. I just want them to go away."

"Do you think that retreating back to your brain and living in your head is going to make all those blockages go away? They will still be there hidden in the shadows."

"Yeah, but at least I won't have to feel all the pressure deep inside my heart that is there now!"

"Adam, the blockages will still be contaminating the field of your heart and coloring your perceptions. When you return to feel your heart again, they will continue to filter and dilute the way that the gentleness of Love can radiate. They will keep you from being an instrument the way you've been designed."

"I hear you and remember you said that all my blockages have to go. But I am scared. And I'm afraid that I'll get stuck in the muck."

"The part of you that has doubts and is scared is the part of you, Adam, that does not trust the True Source of Love," he said kindly. "If you choose the gentleness of Love, you will not be let down. Really, I promise, love will not let you down."

"How do I choose Love?" I asked.

"You already know that. As you feel and gratefully enjoy the gentleness and feel the gentleness radiating, you are choosing Love. When you focus on the pressure or negative emotions surfacing, then you are choosing your pain over Love. Remember, the fact that these blockages have surfaced is a very wonderful sign. It means you have already been trusting Love and it has brought you into the deeper inner layers of your heart. Much cleansing of your heart has already taken place. Now you have come face to face with the bigger blockages that are deeper in your heart because love is pushing against the edges of them. The True Source of Unconditional Love wants to give you the best and wants to remove these blockages for you. All you have to do is keep enjoying the gentleness of Love. That will take care of everything and dissolve the blockages."

"I guess I hit a plateau."

"Yes, you have, Adam, and a huge opportunity awaits you. I suggest that you be careful to stay on the highway."

Chapter Forty-Eight
RESOLUTION CALLS

"Adam, I had a wonderful dream last night. I awoke feeling very happy."

"What was the dream about?"

"I feel it would be better if I shared it with you another time."

"If you say so. What would you like to do today?"

"Why don't you ask your heart what you would like to do, Adam."

"Well, I thought maybe we . . . "

"Adam, you are not catching my drift."

"Well, what do you mean?"

"What I mean is you are being called, but you are not hearing the call."

"Who's calling me? My mother?"

"It's not your mother, Adam. Check in with your heart and listen for a while."

Grandfather walked away. I relaxed and began to enjoy my heart. A feeling came to me that it is time to visit Resolution. I began to feel a magnetic attraction. Yes, Resolution is calling me. Or maybe I'm calling her. I decided to pay her a visit and rest upon her solid rock lap. I found Grandfather sitting on the porch.

"Grandfather, how about we go visit Resolution today?"

"It is best if you visit Resolution by yourself."

"But what will you do?"

"The question is, what will you do, Adam? Will you let the Unconditional Love dissolve your blockages or will you let your blockages retreat back into the shadows?"

"Okay, I'll get ready to go."

"Plan to go for a few days, Adam."

"What?! That's a long time!"

"You will be surprised at how time flies. I have a backpack ready for you with a tent and sleeping bag. Oh, and Adam, be careful not to step on any rattlesnakes," he grinned.

"Thanks a lot. Do you have any other words of wisdom for me?" I joked.

"You will experience two things going on. Deep in your heart you will feel pressure and blockages. You will also feel the gentleness of Love from your heart radiating. If you become focused on the pressure and blockages, they will remain stuck and you will forget to feel the gentleness of Love that wants to give you the best. Always choose being Unconditionally loved over the blockages. You choose Love by enjoying and being grateful. "

"Thanks. Well, I'm off on my adventure," I laughed.

As I walked, my mind began to play games with me. I kept thinking I was about to step on a rattlesnake. But what, at first, looked like snakes to me, were only dead tree limbs lying on the ground.

"Why did he have to go and put that thought in my head?" I complained aloud.

As I approached Resolution, I felt the same magnetic attraction as before. It was pulling me closer. I was happy to see her and could feel that she was welcoming me.

I felt extremely warm from my hike and decided to go for a swim so I took my clothes off and jumped in. Feeling a little self-conscious about getting out of the water, I wondered,"What if someone sees me?" I looked around slowly at the surrounding forest, and then laughed at myself, realizing the only ones who might see me were the squirrels playing in the trees. I climbed out and lay in the sun for awhile.

I spent a long time just listening to the soft sound of the flowing river and being in the peaceful stillness of the moment. After setting up my tent, I built a fire and cooked some rice and lentils. The sun set and the moon was just a sliver in the sky. I stared into the fire and was mesmerized by the sound of the crickets. Then I noticed the lightening bugs blinking on an off in the space that surrounded me.

While relaxing and letting the gentleness of Love bring me into my heart, I began to feel pressure and blockages just like I did the day before. A strong, raw, fiery hot feeling began to surface in my solar plexus. "Not now," I said to myself. I began to think of superficial things in order to get myself into my head and out of my heart. I felt relieved to have pulled away from the internal pressure, although I could feel how it was waiting in the background to emerge whenever I was willing to feel my heart. "Time to sleep," I thought. "I'll regroup in the morning."

135

Chapter Forty-Nine
FACING MY BIGGEST BLOCKAGES

As soon as I woke up, I could feel my solar plexus brewing like it did the night before. It was as if I had a volcano under immense pressure inside of me with the pressure continuing to build. To my surprise, I felt the gentleness of Love while also being able to feel the pressure. I began to relax into the gentleness and could feel the block surfacing. Then I got scared and whispered to myself, "I think I've had enough." Instantly the blockage subsided.

" I'm glad that's over. I think its time to go pick some wild berries." Then I felt my heart call out, "Everything that is not of Love has to go so that you can become an instrument for the True Source of Love." I ignored the call of my heart, climbed down from Resolution's lap and began looking around for a berry patch. But I knew walking away was a cop-out. I had failed to face the opportunity before me and without returning to do so, the blockages and I would remain stuck. However, I was incredibly fearful of facing those deep blockages. "What if my emotions explode and I go off the deep end? What if rage surfaces and I cannot get it back under control?" Then it was as if I could feel the Gift of Unconditional Love calling me back to Resolution, like a loving mother reassuring her scared child that everything will be alright.

I went back and climbed up onto Resolution's lap again. I took at least ten minutes to deeply relax and defuse the built up anxiety and fear. Smiling to my heart, I gratefully enjoyed being loved and cared for. I could feel the gentleness of Love radiating. I began smiling to the hearts of all beings so that I could be an instrument the way that Grandfather taught me. I began to feel the deep blockages surfacing and I asked for the True Source of Love to remove everything keeping me from being an instrument exactly as I was designed to be.

All of a sudden I began to feel deep anger, like hot lava boiling up from a volcano. Layers of anger, resentment, and rage toward my father surfaced. As I relaxed and let the gentleness of Love remove these layers, I could feel those emotions dissolve. I realized my father played a role just as I had played the role of his son. These were merely the parts we played in the drama of our lives. I let the True Source of Unconditional Love help me to forgive him for not being a nurturing father. I began to experience him as a fellow sibling in the journey of life.

Whatever anger I had just experienced and cleared was just the beginning. Something very dark and deep began to emerge from the inner layers of my heart. I could feel that the blockages were hiding in the shadows in the back and bottom of my non-physical heart. I felt that these were old blockages, and I did not know what they were. It felt like pus coming out of an infected wound. Surprisingly, the pus was anger and rage toward God. Somewhere from very deep down, I felt I had been abandoned and rejected by God. A part of me felt so unlovable. It became clear why a part of me strongly resisted accepting Unconditional Love the way Grandfather does. Shaking, trembling, and feeling enraged, I just wanted to ring someone's neck. My trembling and outrage began to escalate, and it felt like I was going to burst. I let out a scream that came from the pit of my gut. That scream went on and on, breath after long breath. I bent over with my head between my legs and lost all track of time, forgetting even where I was. It started to rain. I became aware of every cold drop hitting my bare skin and began to weep and weep. My tears mixed with the raindrops and blended together in a stream that washed over my body. I felt raw. My wounds were open and draining.

Then I remembered what Grandfather told me. If we become focused on the pressure and blockages, they will remain stuck, and we will forget to remain connected to the True Source of Love that is always present to give us the best of the best. He said to always choose the gentleness of Love over the blockages, and that we choose the Gift of Unconditional Love by being grateful for our heart's connection.

I relaxed more while feeling the true heart feelings. As these blockages were erupting, I could now feel the gentleness of Love radiating. More and more aspects of me began to feel loved like I never allowed before. I began to feel the gentleness dissolving the edges of the hurt and anger along with the painful emotions of believing I was rejected and abandoned by God. Yet another part of me was holding onto these blockages. I remember Grandfather sharing with me that cleansing blockages is easy if we are willing to let them go. I began to relax even more, and could feel the Source of Love cleansing everything at a faster rate. Enough tears to fill a cup continued to pour down over my face, though at the same time, I was grateful and could feel the blockages being removed layers at a time. After my anger and feelings of abandonment dissolved, I felt deep guilt, shame and inadequacy emerge. I realized how much these emotions limited my ability to be an instrument for the True Source of Love. These layers and blockages were keeping me from opening to a deeper level of accepting and experiencing that we are all unconditionally and completely loved. Still more blockages surfaced. Multiple layers of arrogance, self-righteousness and judgment toward others emerged. As I kept gratefully enjoying the Gift of Unconditional Love, I could feel those layers dissolving too. Deep, terrifying fear began to surface. It felt like I was loosing my identity – the part of me that was invested in all of the roles I've played. As the gentleness of Love dissolved those blockages I began to laugh uncontrollably. My previous mental creations began to feel absurd. Who I used to think I was began to dissolve, and it all seemed to be a funny joke. At times I felt increased pressure building, and I realized that was because I was holding and not letting go, so I kept relaxing and letting the True Source of Love remove everything of my false identity.

It was so beautiful when I felt the back and bottom of my non-physical heart open. Now the gentleness of Love was radiating simultaneously through the front, back, top, bottom, left and right sides of the heart and it felt that I was free from all edges and borders. The walls and restrictive boundaries I carried for so long had just crumbled. I had held up these walls because I was under the illusion that they were in my best interest and that they were somehow protecting me. The delusion of thinking I need to guard myself from being hurt was so clear....and it seemed like a big joke. I began to feel so unconditionally loved with such complete and sweet tenderness. I felt hugged with the deepest feelings of being soothed, comforted, and totally accepted. I rested like a baby while being embraced in the arms of the Love. I felt the complete and all forgiving Love that is always present for every one of us, no matter what we have ever done. And yes, I could feel that this was not ordinary love, or human love... it was truly Unconditional Love. An Absolute Love that has been present throughout time for every being even during our darkest moments. Yet it was us with our walls, boundaries, fears and need to control or seek power that deluded us. The Gift of Unconditional Love has always been present for every one of us... but we are the ones who turned away.

Previously, I thought it was so wonderful when I was able to feel that my heart was connected to the True Source of Love. A new shift happened, and now I experienced that my whole heart, whole being and physical form was inside the Source of Love....and I no longer experienced myself as living in separation. This is the Gift that Unconditional Love offers us. I realized that living with our whole being inside of the joyful gentleness of Love is where we are meant to be. It was not anything I could achieve by my doing, effort or best intentions. It was all given and happened only when I let the Source of Love dissolve my resistance to being loved completely. Only then was I able to more fully accept being loved without blocking this beautiful process. I wept as I realized that the True Source of Love is waiting to give every one of us the best of the best. It is our effort, and our trying that blocks us from being able to let the gentleness of Love dissolve the separation that we created.

I felt like a lost child who had been found and brought Home. Finally, after being separated for so long, it was as if I was tucked into a warm bed to rest and I knew from the core of my being, that it is all a Gift of Unconditional Love.

Chapter Fifty
RESTING WITHIN THE GIFT OF UNCONDITIONAL LOVE

When I awoke in the morning I quickly realized that my whole heart, whole being and physical form was still immersed within the joyful gentleness of Love. I was surprised to realize that even while sleeping, I was being lovingly embraced.

I began to reflect over my life. I realized how I used to think that living in my head along with all of its rationalizations, excuses, judgments, pushed buttons, and emotional reactivity was normal. Living as a dominant mind, feeling separate, defending my turf, and striving to get somewhere, was what I thought was real and important. Believing the dream, I never realized the perpetual trance that played out in my life.

When I first met Grandfather, I began to feel how beautiful it was to experience my heart. Much of my previous drama and world view dissolved. Yet, at that time, the connection with my heart was temporary. I would only feel it when I let go of the grip of my dominant mind. When my mind started acting like the captain of the ship, I could no longer feel the gentleness of Love radiating from my heart.

Now effortlessly enjoying my heart felt like a permanent Home. My whole being felt that it was naturally resting in the gentleness of Love. I never imagined that this freedom could feel so amazingly wonderful. While feeling immensely grateful, I realized that we are all meant to live a heart-centered life. Only then could the deepest purpose of our existence be fulfilled. While being instruments we all become team players in service for the highest good to happen.

I laughed with joy when I realized that when our whole being is effortlessly resting within a direct connection with the gentleness of Love, was what normal is supposed to feel like. I felt like I awoke from a dream.

While spending the next couple of days picking berries, swimming and relaxing in the sun, I kept remembering how the True Source of Love brought me so sweetly to where I was in that moment.

It was time to return to the LotusHeart cabin. I looked forward to sharing my experience with Grandfather. I said farewell to Resolution .

I enjoyed the walk back while smiling to the trees and wildlife. This time, none of the fallen branches looked like rattlesnakes. I did see a harmless striped garter snake. I picked her up, and she slithered through my fingers. Her tongue darted in and out, and I laughed as I marveled over the wonders of nature.

Chapter Fifty-One
WAKING FROM THE DREAM
OF THE WORLD

Approaching the waterfall back at the LotusHeart cabin at about sunset, I was surprised to find Grandmother Gabriella had arrived from the city during my absence. She and Grandfather were sitting on the warm rocks with their feet in the water.

"Adam! Welcome back!" Grandfather called out.

"Hello, Adam," said Grandmother Gabriella with a warm smile.

"It's good to see you both," I said.

Grandmother Gabriella got up and walked up the hill to the cabin. She returned a few minutes later with a birthday cake she had baked. I told them it was not my birthday. Grandfather said it was a celebration for the birth of my new awakening. I felt tears come to my eyes as they sang "Happy Birthday."

"Adam," she said, "We are congratulating you on your waking from the dream of the world!"

"How can you tell?" I asked.

"It's so wonderful to feel the joyful gentleness of Love radiating sweetly and freely from your being," she said. "Your heart now knows that every human is your sibling and humanity is our family."

"Yes," I shared, "And it is so clear that it's all a Gift of Unconditional Love. I did not do anything but let love remove all the garbage I had collected. This is all beyond anything I ever could have imagined!"

"Adam," said Grandfather, "We understand, and we are so grateful that you have realized how the Gift of Unconditional Love is present in every moment to give every person the best of the best. It is beyond the greatest romantic love or anything we can imagine. It is an all-encompassing Love that is complete, and so beyond anything that the human mind can ever conceive. Only the Gift of Unconditional Love can bring us Home to who we really are. When the ego ran the show, we created a lot of junk in the form of blockages and densities that were accumulated in our heart. Finally, we are letting the Source of Love clean up the mess so the "real us" can be free."

141

Grandfather chuckled with delight. He then stared into my eyes with a piercing compassionate gaze while smiling so sweetly and freely. As long as I live, I will never forget his radiant eyes and his sweet smile.

"Adam... I'm so glad you remembered my parting words."

"But how do you know I did, Grandfather?"

"When you left to visit Resolution you had one eye open and one eye closed. The eye that was open was the part of you that had partially awakened from the dream of the world, but there was still another part of you in deep trance. Your wounds, blockages and your colored lenses were keeping you stuck. In our time together you had glimpses of awakening, but you were not yet willing to let Love pierce the veil and remove your deeper blockages. Now you have, and both of your eyes are open. In the dream I had a few nights ago I heard Resolution calling you, and I saw you awake from the trance of the dominant mind. I felt so very happy. Now you can live in the world as an instrument .... and without getting lost in the world. You are now able to live a heart-centered life."

"Thank you, Grandfather. I didn't know what I was in for, but Resolution provided such a safe space for me."

Grandmother Gabriella smiled

"What an amazing birthday gift!" I said again. "I feel so grateful. Grandfather, are those tears of joy trickling from your eyes?"

"Yes, Adam. They are joyful tears. I am happy to feel how your whole being is within the gentleness of Love, and you are living as a heart which happens to have a physical body."

"Grandfather Sage has guided you well," said Grandmother Gabriella. "I couldn't have done better myself," she laughed.

In the morning, I got dressed, took a basket from the kitchen and crept quietly out of the cabin. Several types of wild berries were in season, and I thought I'd surprise Grandfather and Grandmother Gabriella with some for breakfast. I returned a short time later and found Grandmother Gabriella in the kitchen, making tea.

"Adam, they're beautiful. Thank you," she said, taking the basket. "I can tell they were picked with love while you were feeling grateful."

"It is nice to hear you two talking," said Grandfather, as he entered the kitchen. "Adam, you are ready to return to your mom's house today?"

"I am not sure. I really feel like I'd rather stay here with you both."

"I can understand that Adam, though your lessons here are completed. Now it is time to return to your community to be an instrument. You will have more fun than you've ever had before! It will be a new type of fun, though, because now you will be able to live in the world without getting sucked into the drama of the world. Listen carefully. Remember to always give all credit to the True Source of Unconditional Love for all wonderful things, as well as for your achievements or accomplishments."

"I will, Grandfather. Thank you so much for everything."

The three of us sat quietly smiling at each other's hearts.

"Grandfather, I don't know how to say good-bye or to thank you enough. Words cannot describe what I feel."

"I understand, Adam. The depth of our sibling connection is beyond words."

"This feels like my earth home. I don't feel like leaving."

"Adam, remember your true Home is within the gentleness of Love, and that will exist wherever you are. Thank you for being my dear brother. Where you go from here is all part of the plan, just as our summer together was part of that plan. Remember, that from time to time you will get pulled into emotions or judgments, but you will not stay gone from your heart because now you can easily, effortlessly and joyfully realize who you are not, and let the gentleness of Love bring you back Home to who you truly are. The core of your heart realizes that embracing the spiritual dimension of life is directly related to accepting the Gift of Unconditional Love."

Chapter Fifty-Two
ITS ALL THE GIFT OF UNCONDITIONAL LOVE

When I got home and unpacked my clothes, I came across my journal from the summer. I turned to the first page and there were the five principles Grandfather had given me.

Number One:

The True Source of Unconditional Love is the Source of our true heart feelings

Number Two:

The True Source of Unconditional Love is the Source of our life

Number Three:

The True Source of Unconditional Love is always present to give us the best

Number Four:

Our deepest purpose on earth is to be an instrument through our connection with the True Source of Unconditional Love

Number Five:

Living a heart-centered life and relying on the True Source of Unconditional Love, will bring us Home to who we really are.

When Grandfather first shared these five principles with me, they seemed so foreign and way out. I thought Grandfather was from another world, and I questioned whether he was crazy. Now I realize he was a great gift to support me in waking up and learning to live with my heart and mind in alignment.

It is interesting to be with my mother. On one hand, I still see her as my mother, but I also relate to her as a fellow sibling in the classroom of life. Previously I was locked in a power struggle with her. Now I know she just has her role to play in earth school and is doing the best she can. I will continue to play the role of the son, just as there are many other roles to play in life. Yet my true being is beyond all the roles I play, and it is such a freeing experience. It is wonderful that I do not get emotionally triggered like I used to and can accept her as she is, another sibling on the path just like me.

These many roles that we play with the people in our lives provide wonderful opportunities to learn how to live a heart-centered life. Every moment is a choice point to choose the gentleness of Love over our right to become judgmental or emotionally reactive. When we get triggered and react with our dominant mind, we fail to learn our greatest lessons. But when we let our heart's connection with the True Source of Unconditional Love give us the best of the best, we learn to let this sacred connection bring us back into heart-centered alignment.

Experiencing my whole heart and whole being within the gentleness of Love has changed my outlook on everything. Instead of just thinking and seeing the world through my mind's eye, I am able to think and see the world through the doorway of my heart.

When both my eyes were closed, I saw the world only in the way I had been taught and conditioned to see it. My blockages and wounds colored my vision and contaminated the field of my heart. I failed to see how my own conditioning created the illusions that kept me in the trances of everyday life.

I now know that when we are in the trance of the world, it's as if there's a special day we are awaiting when all will be perfect. But that is like chasing a pie in the sky. We fail to realize the moment is always here and now. This is why it is so important that we let the True Source of Unconditonal Love remove everything that is not of Love, so that the real us can awaken. This is the key to embracing the spiritual dimension of life. Only then can our true nature be revealed as we live our life on earth as an instrument.

Thank you for taking the time to read my story about how I came to let Love open my heart. The True Source of Love is calling the core of every heart. We are collectively moving together. And it is all the Gift of Unconditional Love... the complete Unconditional Love for you, me and everyone.

Questions for Self-Refection and Sharing

1. The Introduction of the book explains how our heart is special and how our heart is the key for making each moment the most special and precious gift it can be? *How do you feel about how this Introduction explains the important role our heart plays in experiencing happiness and fulfillment?*

2. In Chapter 4, Grandfather told Adam, "Life itself is your great teacher and your classroom. What if I told you that you are on earth to learn to become who you really are, not to remain who you think or believe you are or what other people have told you about yourself or want you to be. Unless you learn to live a heart-centered life, you will never be able to find the real you." *How do you feel about what Grandfather shared with Adam?*

3. As described in Chapter 5, how do you feel about falling in holes and how is this like the biography of many people's lives? *In what way does this relate to you or others you know?*

4. In Chapter 7, Grandfather outlined five principles he called the foundation of learning in the classroom of life. *How do you relate about these principles?*

5. In Chapter 8 Grandfather explained that the voice of life that often becomes our greatest teacher is our own mental and emotional pain and that our pain acts as a signal to inform us that we are not in harmony or connected properly to our heart. *Do you agree and if so, in what ways does this relate to your life.*

6. In Chapter 9, there is a distinction made between emotion reactivity and an overly dominant mind compared to true heart feelings which grandfather calls the natural expressions of your heart. *What does this mean to you?*

7. In Chapter 10, the metaphor of how clouds block the radiance of the sun is explored. *How do you feel this is related to the blockage of our true heart feelings and the limited patterns our mind creates?*

8. In Chapter 11, Grandfather confronted Adam and said, "The weeds of your mind, Adam. You feast on them and you don't even know it.

When you live with a dominant mind, weeds grow and you eat them throughout the day. Not only that, you become just like the weeds and at times even grow thorns." *In what way does this relate to your personal life?*

9. In Chapter 12, Grandfather stated, "You cannot keep a bird from flying over your head, but you sure can prevent it from building a nest in your hair." *How do you feel about the explanation of this metaphor and can you see any ways it has applied to your life?*

10. In Chapter 13, Grandfather alludes to the notion that we are brainwashed and tells Adam, "Sex and money are the cosmic joke. Depending on them for contentment will send you on a wild goose chase. There is no saying where that ride could lead you, but one thing is sure – it is a dead end road. People have been falling in that hole and getting themselves in trouble throughout the history of humankind." *How do you feel about this idea of a "wild goose chase" in life? Have you ever found yourself on a wild goose chase and if so what was that like?*

11. In Chapter 14, Grandfather likes to view "obstacles as opportunities" and Adam first expressed his opinion of obstacles being as a "pain in the ass." *What is your view on obstacles?*

12. One of Adam's initial break through takes place in Chapter 16 noted by Grandfather stating to Adam, "You are beginning to realize how when faced with the same situation, you perceive things one way with your head and a different way with your heart." *Does this have meaning to you?*

13. In Chapter 19, Grandfather states, "Most people live with at least an ongoing low grade activation of their fight/flight mechanism. They do not ever get to the point in feeling 'I have arrived and everything is wonderful'. They are on the go to the next thing and the next thing. Often, even if everything seems okay, there is a part of them waiting for the other shoe to drop. Or they seem to always think about what comes next." *Can you relate to this and if so how?*

14. In Chapter 21, it states, "A done deal is a done deal. Would it make sense to argue with a done deal and expect the circumstances to change?" *Have you ever argued with a 'done deal' and if so, where did that lead you?*

15. In Chapter 22, there was a crisis. Adam stated, "I realized I was really stuck in my head. I remembered grandfather telling me that when we are in our head, we believe our story to be real and true. I wondered how the story and all the pain I was feeling would be if I was in my heart." *Can you relate to a time when you were stuck in your head and believed something to be true, and now realize it was a limited perception?*

16. In Chapter 23, Grandfather shared, "Adam, if you study your life, you will see you have played both roles. By finding fault in others it allows you to feel more secure in your own position. When you are feeling more-than another you feel superior, or better, than another person. When you feel less-than another you are feeling insecure or inadequate." *In what ways can you relate to this?*

17. One of the keys to the book found in Chapter 24 is based on the understanding that innate wisdom exists because of the connection between our heart and the True Source of Unconditional Love. *How do you feel about the idea of innate wisdom and how it can guide us to make wise decisions?*

18. In Chapter 25, Healthy Boundaries, Adam comes to the realization that, "One day my boundaries with my mother were enmeshed. Every little thing she did or said pissed me off. The next day I disengaged, and when she spoke to me, I nodded and said 'uh huh,' but didn't hear a word she said." *Do enmeshed or disengaged boundaries apply to your life and if so how does this affect your relationships?*

19. Grandfather asked Adam in Chapter 26, "Of all choices, what do you feel is the greatest choice we can make?" Adam, responded, "I feel it's to choose to live a heart-centered life instead of living stuck in our head." *How do you feel about Adam's response?*

20. Grandfather explained in Chapter 27, "If a person has not developed the peaceful, calm reference point of the heart, then they may not recognize when they are out of tune." and "The point is, it is crucial that we develop an internal reference point to minimize the mistakes we make through our words, thoughts and actions." *What does this mean to you?*

21. In Chapter 28, Adam got himself into some trouble by making a

poor choice. *Did you feel Grandfather should have left Adam in jail for the night or was this a mistake on his part?*

22. In Chapter 29, Grandfather tells Adam, "Life is a process, Adam, in which we learn to wake up from the trances of everyday life and learn to live a heart-centered life. Emotional trances interfere with our ability to live in harmony. And you re-create trances when you allow your head to be your home." *What ways do your recognize in your life where you tend to recreate certain emotional patterns?*

23. In Chapter 30, Adam came to realize, "We don't always see as clearly as we think we're seeing. We think we're seeing and experiencing the world as it is, but in reality we're only seeing the world as it's reflected through the colored lenses of our mind." *Can you relate to Adam's realization and if so, in what ways?*

24. In Chapter 31, Grandfather makes a distinction between heartfullness and mindfulness, and explains that mindfulness can lead to a plateau in terms of how we are able to enjoy our heart. *In terms of how this is described, how do you feel about the difference between heartfullness and mindfulness?*

25. Grandfather tells Adam in Chapter 32, "The Gift of Unconditional Love always wants to give us the best. Only we separate ourselves because we have chosen to live in our head. The True Source of Love is always willing to help us by removing everything that is not for our highest good." *How do you feel about this? Does this ring true to your heart?*

26. In Chapter 33, Grandfather explains about the heart zone, the caution zone, and the danger zone. *How do you feel about these and how does it apply to your life?*

27. In Chapter 34, Adam faces the dilemma of feeling "trapped between two worlds." *Can you relate to his experience in any time during your life and if so in what way?*

28. The idea of "synchronicities" is discussed in Chapter 35, and Grandfather said, "It was not by chance that our paths crossed." *Can you relate to the concept of synchronicity and have you ever felt that meeting someone was not a coincidence?*

29. In Chapter 35, Grandfather shared about the risk of how, "A dominant mind will lead you into all kinds of dead end traps. Then you become convinced that the dead end you are following is really leading you somewhere important. People often spend their entire lives doing this, and fail to realize what they are looking for all along is simply their own heart. Adam, let's be realistic. You are going to get sidetracked from time to time. There are lessons to learn on these off-track adventures. That is okay because it is all part of the journey. There are always lessons in what we call mistakes." *In what ways have you found yourself on a dead-end street and realized it was not as important as you thought or that the path was detrimental? Do you feel that there are lessons in what we call mistakes, and if so, how?*

30. In Chapter 36, Grandfather explains to Adam, "We each have our own unique set of wounds. We all have our own stories. When we do not heal our wounds, we carry them around with us and they affect how we see things, and how we feel and react to life." *How do you feel about this? How do your emotional reactions or people's emotional reactions toward you relate to what Grandfather shared?*

31. A big shift for Adam occurred when he met Grandfather's friend John. In Chapter 38, Adam finally realized the temporary nature of the brain and that the brain is not the source of who we are. *How did you respond to his conclusion and how do you feel about that?*

32. Adam was introduced to "Resolution" in Chapter 39. *Do you have your own version of "Resolution" that is a safe space for you and if so where is it?*

33. In Chapter 40 Grandfather shared, "One of the keys to a fulfilling life is overcoming the distinction between what you consider a chore and what you consider a reward. The best reward that you can reap is when you are heartfully engaged with gratitude in whatever you are doing." and, "Life becomes much more entertaining when we stop separating work from rewards, Adam. Rewards provide only temporary pleasure. If you have not figured that out, much of your life will seem like a burden." *How do you feel about what Grandfather shared with Adam?*

34. It was explained in Chapter 41, "Adam, the quality of your thoughts when your head is in charge, is very different from the qual-

ity of your thoughts when you are heart centered. A lot of our problems and burdens are created and sustained by the kinds of thoughts we think and emotions we experience when we are mind dominant." *How do you feel about this understanding?*

35. In Chapter 42, Grandfather shared the following metaphor. "Adam, if a loving mother has two children and one child stays clean and the other child always gets dirty in the mud, doesn't the mother still love the child who gets dirty? And doesn't the mother want to pick up the child from the mud and clean him, cuddle him, and tuck him into a warm bed?" *What does this metaphor mean to you?*

36. Grandfather shared in Chapter 43, "We are not here on earth to gather, conquer or achieve more and more. We are here to be instruments for the True Source of Love. It is our birthright, and it is our ultimate purpose. Let us be grateful for even the smallest of things." *In what ways does hearing this effect how you feel right now?*

37. Grandfather explained in Chapter 45, "This is a paradox, Adam. People think they are vulnerable if they open their heart and that by staying closed hearted and head strong, they are assuming a safe position that will protect them. It is actually the opposite. The safest place to be is with an open heart because it is the gentleness of Love that opens our heart. That creates a field around you that protects you from the negative energies which exist in space. When you have a closed heart and a strong head, the gentleness of Love is not radiating so you lack a protective field around you. Negative energies from people or places can enter your field and affect you in ways you are not aware of. The real risk is to live with a closed heart." *How do you feel about this and how open do you feel about letting the gentleness of Love open your heart?*

38. In Chapter 46, Grandfather shared, "As you become more and more grounded in your heart, you can consciously experience the essence of your being. Your true self, the real you, your spirit, resides in the core of your heart. Our journey is about waking up and being who we really are. All the roles we act out in life are simply roles we play, but the roles are not the real us. People fail to realize this and become identified with these roles. Our true self is beyond all of those roles, yet while we are living in the world, we get to learn lessons from the assortment of roles we play. Whether the role is as a son, brother,

student, father, husband, worker, boss, friend, neighbor, leader, or follower, these roles provide wonderful opportunities. Every moment is a chance to choose to gratefully enjoy and accept the Gift of Unconditional Love, so that our hearts can open more." *What does this really mean to you and how does it affect how you view life?*

39. In Chapter 47, Adam shared he was scared to face his unresolved emotions that were buried deep. Grandfather responded, "I do understand your fears and concerns very well because I went through them myself. Before your head convinces you that it is safe to retreat to the mind-dominant way of thinking, I would like to share something. Everyone is looking for their heart, yet they do not realize it. They continue to look for Love in the wrong places as the old song says. They endeavor to find happiness and joy through people, places or things – all temporary pleasures and they confuse them with authentic happiness. They fail to find the happiness and joy that only our hearts can experience. There is nothing wrong with the material world but when you expect or look toward it for your fulfillment, it will lead you down dead end streets with lots of holes in the road along the way." *What does this mean to you and can you see any ways it applies to your life?*

40. In Chapter 48, before Adam left for Resolution, he asked Grandfather for any words of wisdom. Grandfather replied, "You will experience two things going on. Deep in your heart you will feel pressure and blockages. You will also feel the gentleness of Love from your heart radiating. If you become focused on the pressure and blockages, they will remain stuck and you will forget to feel the gentleness of Love that wants to give you the best. Always choose being Unconditionally Loved over the blockages. You choose Love by enjoying and being grateful." *How do you feel about what Grandfather shared with Adam?*

41. In Chapter 49, Adam went through a profound transformation at Resolution, and came to realize that, "The Gift of Unconditional Love has always been present for every one of us...but we are the ones who turn away." *How do you feel about this and Adams spiritual transformation?*

42. After Adam's transformation, in Chapter 50, he shared, "I began to reflect over my life. I realized how I used to think that living in

my head along with all of its rationalizations, excuses, judgments, pushed buttons, and emotional reactivity was normal. Living as a dominant mind, feeling separate, defending my turf, and striving to get somewhere, was what I thought was real and important. Believing the dream, I never realized the perpetual trance that played out in my life." *How do you feel about the different patterns and ways that you create distress in your life? How do you feel about learning to live a more joyful heart-centered life that becomes your new normal?*

43. In Chapter 51, Grandmother Gabriella shared with Adam, "It's so wonderful to feel the gentleness of Love radiating sweetly and freely from your being. Your heart now knows that every human is your sibling and humanity is our family." *How does that make you feel and do you agree that humanity is our family?*

44. In Chapter 52, Adam returns home and experiences his mother from a totally different perspective. He shares, "It is interesting to be with my mother. On one hand, I still see her as my mother, but I also relate to her as a fellow sibling in the classroom of life. Previously I was locked in a power struggle with her. Now I know she just has her role to play in earth school and is doing the best she can. I will continue to play the role of the son, just as there are many other roles to play in life. Yet my true being is beyond all the roles I play, and it is such a freeing experience. It is wonderful that I do not get emotionally triggered like I used to and can accept her as she is, another sibling on the path just like me." *How do you feel about the transformation Adam has made and that he perceives his mother beyond the role of her being his mother?*

45. The five principles which were the foundation of the book are:

1. The True Source of Unconditional Love is the Source of our true heart feelings
2. The True Source of Unconditional Love is the Source of our life
3. The True Source of Unconditional Love is always present to give us the best
4. Our deepest purpose on earth is to be an instrument through our connection with the True Source of Unconditional Love
5. Living a heart-centered life and relying on the Source of Love, will bring us Home to who we really are.

Now that you have completed the book, how do you feel about these five principles that became the foundation of Adam's spiritual and transformational experience?

46. *Do you believe it is possible for someone like Adam to go through the kind of personal and spiritual growth transformation he went through?*

47. *How do you feel about being able to go through a similar spiritual transformation?*

48. *Now that you have completed the book, how important do you feel it is to live a heart-centered life?*

49. *How do you feel living with our heart and mind in alignment is related to fulfilling the spiritual dimension of life?*

50. *What are the key lessons you have learned from this book that are the most meaningful to you?*

HEART BASED INSTITUTE

About Heart Based Institute

Heart Based Institute is a 501(c)(3) nonprofit organization committed to inspiring positive change through delivering ground-breaking and proven-effective heart based educational workshops and professional training programs, community outreach, and research initiatives. Our specific heart based approach is rooted in the premise that every person has the capacity to experience profound transformational changes when the heart and mind come into healthy alignment. By viewing each person as a "whole being" rather than as a symptom or problem, and teaching a simple and effective means of achieving heart-mind alignment, we are transforming lives, organizations and communities around the world.

Heart Based Therapeutics™ is a transformative, state-of-the-art modality focused on learning to enjoy the many benefits of heart-centered living. Combining psychological theory with experiential learning, Heart Based Therapeutics™ provides an insightful, practical and enjoyable heart based approach to reducing stress and burnout, improving the quality of interpersonal relationships, and enhancing professional efficacy within the workplace. Learning to enhance the experience of peace, calm, gratitude, and joy directly optimizes all aspects of living as well as develops psychological resiliency for effectively adapting to adversity and stressors. When one learns to feel safe living with an open heart, a profound healing transformation can occur which leads to a tangible experience of completeness, contentment and fulfillment.

For more information, visit: heartbased.org

About Ed Rubenstein, Ph.D.

Ed Rubenstein, Ph.D. is the Director of Education and Professional Training Programs for Heart Based Institute. He is also a licensed psychologist who has been at the forefront of the human potential field for over 35 years. Ed received his Doctorate in Counseling Psychology from Florida State University, and holds a Masters in Rehabilitation Counseling from Florida State University, a Masters in Psychology from Radford University, and a Masters in Spiritual Studies from Goddard College. Over the course of his career, he has worked with a multiplicity of client populations and has conducted workshops and trainings for federal, city and county agencies as well as university, hospital, non-profit, corporate, and community settings.

Ed's focus within psychology is on a heart based approach and its impact on the psychological and relational well-being of his diverse clientele. His transformative approach to psychology demonstrates a natural way for developing resiliency, emotional management, and for building positive relationships. Facilitating professional workshops internationally, Ed shares his insights and in-depth knowledge about living a heart-centered life, supported by tools and approaches that contribute to a deeper experience of personal fulfillment. He has successfully presented workshops at the National Institutes of Health (NIH), Pan American World Health Organization (PAHO), and other agencies.

Ed lives in the Blue Ridge Mountains with his wife; they have two grown sons. He can be contacted at ed@heartbased.org

CPSIA information can be obtained
at www.ICGtesting.com
Printed in the USA
FFOW01n1718250318
45913689-46838FF